T0001023

MOM YOUR WAY

YASMIN KADERALI

CEO of Mommy's Bliss

MOM YOUR WAY

JUDGMENT-FREE
WISDOM TO EMPOWER NEW MOMS

FLASH POINT

Copyright © 2024 by Mandala Mom Media, LLC

All rights reserved.

No part of this book may be reproduced, or stored in a retrieval system, or transmitted in any form or by any means, electronic, mechanical, photocopying, recording, or otherwise, without express written permission of the publisher.

Quote by Dr. Raveen Gogia courtesy of the author.
Quote by Christine Noa Sterling used by permission.
Quote by Nicole Kumi courtesy of the author.

Published by Flashpoint™ Books, Seattle
www.flashpointbooks.com

Produced by Girl Friday Productions

Cover design: Emily Weigel
Production editorial: Abi Pollokoff
Project management: Kristin Duran

Image credits (SS denotes Shutterstock): Cover, ix, 1, 59, 65, 84, 87, 107, 121, 127: ViSnezh/SS (mandala); front cover, i, iii, v, viii: Fouboud/SS (mandala); back cover, 127–128: Jessica Stout Paul; xi, xiv: Carol Vaziri; xii: Cat Fennell; 3, 74: ya_blue_ko/ SS (hand), Jesi Maakad (button); 5: BRO.vector/SS; 6, 66: ivector/SS; 9, 42, 89, 116, 120: GoodStudio/SS; 11: anna.spoka/SS (mirror), Alena Nv/SS (high five); 14, 19–22, 60, 70, 105: Jesi Maakad; 15: Olian_Rosa/SS; 16: VectorsMarket/SS; 24: Stesy/SS; 29: Elena Pimukova/SS; 32, 46, 102: Matiushenko Yelyzaveta/SS; 35: Bass Tatiana/ SS; 38: Vector by/SS; 45: Tanya Shanahina/SS; 56: Undrey/SS; 77: Olga Strel/SS; 79: Bibadash/SS (moms), GoodStudio/SS (dad); 81: Anna Krestiannykova/SS; 97: janna_t/SS (luggage), GoodStudio/SS (mom), lemono/SS (child); 101: Flash Vector/SS; 108: Visual Generation/SS; 117: Edge Creative/SS (blocks, dinosaur, train), happpy.designer/SS (basket, shoes)

Limit of Liability / Disclaimer of Warranty: The Publisher and author make no representation or warranties with respect to the accuracy or completeness of the contents of this work and specifically disclaim all warranties, including without limitation warranties of fitness for a particular purpose. No warranty may be created or extended by sales or promotional materials. The advice and strategies contained herein may not be suitable for every situation. The work is sold with the understanding that the Publisher is not engaged in rendering medical, legal, or other professional advice or services. If professional assistance is required, the services of a competent professional person should be sought. Neither the Publisher nor the author shall be liable for damages arising herefrom.

ISBN (paperback): 978-1-959411-52-9
ISBN (ebook): 978-1-959411-53-6

Library of Congress Control Number: 2023915597

First edition

To my two little dudes, Julian and Kiyan, I truly love you more than anything in this world, even donuts, really. Thank you for making me a mom. I can only hope doing this mom thing my way doesn't screw you up.

To Mom and Dad, for putting up with me (with endless support) as I discovered how to do life my way.

To the Mommy's Bliss community, thanks for believing in me and inspiring me to lead like a mom boss.

To any mom who ever questioned or judged me, thank you for reminding me to own my way.

CONTENTS

• • • •

CHAPTER 3 87
THE SIXTH TRIMESTER

CHAPTER 4 107
NOW YOU'RE A MOM . . . FOREVER!

EXTRAS 121

ABOUT THE AUTHOR 127

INTRODUCTION

• • • •

I'll never forget the phone call I got from one of my best friends when his first daughter was born. He said, "Oh my god, Yaz, it was insane . . . She just came out of her body, a little human being, just suddenly here. It was surreal. Why aren't people talking about this all day and every day? How does this happen *all* the time? This was the craziest moment of my life, and I just need to talk about it!"

At the time, I had not yet had kids and was trying to relate, but I could only listen and share his excitement. This "miracle of life" wasn't unfamiliar to me. My mom was a doula and Lamaze coach when I was growing up. She would be prepping for her evening classes and sometimes had to get the videos all cued up on our VHS at dinnertime. I remember rolling my eyes with my brothers and knowing that my mom felt this deep connection to childbirth, but I had no idea why.

It wasn't until I had my first kid that I totally understood the bizarre and miraculous experience of having a human suddenly come out of your body. It *does* feel like an impossible thing! I understood my friend's overwhelming excitement. I understood why my mom had attached to this special moment in a woman's life. It was truly a miracle. And it was the first time I felt super-blissed-out, exhausted, scared, confused, and excited all at once. It was the most unexpected "Welcome to parenthood!" moment I could have imagined. And then, alongside this bundle of emotions, we took our new cutie-pie home, and just as I settled in with my pillows, pads, and ice packs, I thought, *So WTF do I do now?*

In those first moments of my motherhood journey, I had to learn to surrender to all of the unknowns (and that's all parenting is!). A lot of the early moments were a blur, and I can't remember everything I was thinking. (Yes, I feel the guilt of not keeping a journal during those first few months, but I was sleep-deprived and barely able to shower!) Regardless, I do remember thinking a lot about how much my life had changed within moments, and yet everything around me told me to focus on my baby and not on myself. A month in, I asked myself, *Am I even the same person? Am I even doing this mom stuff right?* I had an abundance of questions about my *own* journey of becoming a mom and what that meant, coupled with a lot of hesitation about asking friends or family for advice because of the fear that I would seem selfish to be thinking of myself. Or I would be caught in imposter syndrome, worrying that I didn't actually know what the hell I was doing!

The reality is that *none* of us really knows what we are doing when it comes to being a new mom. Nothing can truly prepare you for all the unknowns of each day, let alone what each hour brings. But this book will help prepare you for some of the transitions that you will soon be (or are) navigating, while reassuring you that you are not alone and you are doing a *great* job, Mama!

I get it. There's almost too much information out there. During my first year postpartum, I often felt overwhelmed the more deeply I dove into reading parenting books, scrolling mommy blogs, and downloading as many new parenting apps

as I could find. I also quickly realized that all the information coming my way was entirely about my baby: feeding schedules, nap
schedules, poop tracking, breast or bottle, the five S's (swad-
dle, side-stomach position, shush, swing, and suck), and sleep
training. Geesh, talk about overload! Don't get me wrong . . . I
loved focusing on my baby, and it kept me out of my head. But
I certainly had moments of *Umm, hi . . . What about me?* I was
uniquely fortunate, though, because I had the team at Mommy's
Bliss always there to answer questions and give real-life parenting insights, and the feedback was consistently compassionate.
There was no judgment or "you should/you shouldn't." But not
everyone has this built-in support community.

Mommy's Bliss is a wellness brand that my mom founded
and passed on to me. We have a team of parents that drives

THE BIRTH OF MOMMY'S BLISS

My mom started our company in 1999. She cared for me and my two brothers while working as a full-time nurse, doula, and lactation consultant. She was immersed in all things "new mom." I saw how much she loved being a part of this new chapter in a woman's life. When she saw new moms struggling with their colicky or fussy baby, she would always recommend gripe water, a liquid herbal supplement that she had known from growing up in Scotland and Tanzania. I would see these moms hugging my mom and thanking her for her suggestion—the gripe water had helped them and allowed them to enjoy more of those first moments.

My mom did not label herself an entrepreneur. Instead, she was driven by compassion. She decided to re-create the traditional gripe water, and worked with a manufacturer who was familiar with

liquid herbal supplements. This way she was able to develop an updated formula that had only simple, natural ingredients and no alcohol, unnecessary additives, or dyes. She felt this was ultimately a better option than the traditional product that was only available as an import. The early years of success were based mostly on word of mouth among moms, doulas, and pediatricians. About ten years into this journey, I joined my mom, initially with the goal of just helping her

out. I had no idea I would fall in love with the brand and become CEO within a few years. By 2011, I knew my parents wanted to retire, and I had developed a passion to grow the company and product line; I saw such potential for the brand to innovate and connect with new moms on many different levels. Even so, my excitement for the brand was nothing compared to my passion that unexpectedly sprang up for the company with the arrival of my first son in 2016. My life and my perception of Mommy's Bliss changed dramatically now that I was a mom. I could now really see the shelf at Target from a mom's eyes; I could feel the nerves when giving my Julian his first vitamins. Suddenly I had a new vision for not only the brand, but the kind of company that celebrated parents and integrated the parental wisdom into our product development, marketing, and company policies. And it worked! The company has grown significantly, and I love the team I work with. The company's DNA is still based on compassion.

the company, including product innovation and marketing, because we have been there, and we get it all! We believe in empowering and supporting moms through all the bliss and the sh*t that comes their way. But this book isn't about Mommy's Bliss. It's about *you*.

My hope is that reading this book feels like you are chatting with your best friend . . . You know, the nonjudgmental one who gets what you are going through and never questions your ordering wine at lunchtime. I want other new moms out there to know and feel that they are growing in the journey too; it's more than okay to focus on yourself and what all this new-mom stuff means to you and your identity.

Also know that thinking ahead about the many new scenarios that are coming can actually be helpful and not purely panic/anxiety-inducing. We can each figure out how "to mom" in our own way and to eventually find the bliss in it all too.

I know how fortunate I was to have a loving partner/husband

by my side during this time and that we were able to have kids easily. I also know that there are many different desires regarding partnership, coparenthood, or single parenthood, and regardless of your situation, this book is a reminder that you can feel empowered to do this *your* way. We all need support from others, but who those people are is up to *you.*

I try to find gratitude in the simple fact that I have two healthy boys, no matter how crazy a parenting day it has been. And I allow myself to feel frustrated and challenged, without discounting how lucky I feel. Figuring out how to hold space in your heart for all these emotions and develop confidence in doing things *your* way is what this book is all about. Although the anecdotes and tips in these pages may refer to my own experience, I hope they will speak to any parent, regardless of gender, age, relationship, and the pathway—IVF, adoption, surrogacy—they took to become parents, because that is what this whole new parenting thing is: an adventure that brings a giant life change and a purpose, with a lot of ups and downs and bumps (and blowout diapers) along the way. I hope this book offers you all the comfort and encouragement you need because, as we all deserve to know about ourselves, no matter what, you are f'ing *amazing*!

You were probably gifted a ton of books and supplies for taking care of your baby, the focus being on the new arrival and related paraphernalia, but *Mom Your Way* is about supporting *you* as you navigate all these new changes and unknowns. For me, there were so many things that weren't talked about in the books or blogs I read. I had questions about the baby (duh), but I also had many questions about myself and how I would cope.

This book will cover:

SLEEP!
If you're consumed with worries about sleep and sleep deprivation (like I was), I've got you.

EMOTIONS, ANXIETY, AND BAGGAGE

What will the emotional roller coaster look like with a baby and hormones? How might my childhood affect the way I parent? Don't worry; we will talk a lot about this.

IDENTITY (AND MOM GUILT)

New moms can catch a case of the "shoulds" in the blink of an eye—don't let this get you down. Reflection prompts throughout this book will help you overcome insecurities, fears, and mom guilt, helping you to embrace your new identity as a mom while still feeling true to yourself.

BODY STUFF

I don't know any mom friend who hasn't struggled with all the weird sh*t that can happen to the body after giving birth. Stay tuned for tips, tricks, and my favorite must-have items to get through all the yuckies.

CHAPTER 1

THE FOURTH TRIMESTER

> **Baby:** From birth to three months
> **You:** Tired, sore, excited, and scared

They're here! And you're alive. Welcome to the fourth trimester, a time when you will experience as much learning about yourself as about your new babe. You've totally got this! It's funny (and by funny, I mean ironic) to be writing a book encouraging you to mom it your way, when the book is basically about giving you unsolicited advice. Just pretend I'm your bestie, and we won't judge each other. But really, it takes listening to others to discover what *your way* is.

So, who am I? My name is Yasmin, and I am the mom of two little dudes: Julian, who is seven years old, and Kiyan, who is five. I am also the CEO of a family wellness brand called Mommy's Bliss, which focuses on the diverse experiences women go through as moms and how to support their own and their children's health and well-being.

The advice and tips in this book are informed by my in-the-trenches experience as a mom and as the CEO of Mommy's Bliss, a position that has provided my brain with a catalog of mommy wisdom and experiences from all the conversations I have had at the office. My Mommy's Bliss coworkers and I have discussed the timing of when each of us would take "pumping" breaks during the day, and we've exchanged tips for boosting our milk supply. At work, over the years I have read thousands of posts from our consumers on social media where they shared their input on our products. I realized and shared that truly every mom and parent has wisdom and experience to share that can help other parents. What I bring to the table is a realness and awareness of the life-changing, epic, and emotional nature of this transition into motherhood that not many people talk about. For me and so many of my friends, this was the most significant change in our lives, and I believe it deserves more acknowledgment and conversation.

Everyone has heard the proverb "It takes a village to raise a child." While I agree with this, our village is very different in 2024. My village includes my family, friends, coworkers at Mommy's Bliss, and various babysitters and helpers. I even consider some of the apps on my phone as part of my support system; they truly help me get supplies for my family and conveniently provide me with access to a wider village. I have also *chosen* my village versus it being passed on to me. This is different from in the past. Today, boundaries can be set; your village can change daily; and the value of emotional connection and support within your village is more important now than ever.

I was so excited to finally become a mom. I knew there were going to be huge changes in myself, my life, and my marriage, changes that I couldn't really prepare for despite any number of new-mommy books or baby apps. What pregnancy taught me and what my motto has become through all this is to surrender. Surrender to it *all*! If it's six o'clock in the evening and you haven't yet showered . . . surrender. If you have been up all night with a colicky baby who just won't rest . . . surrender (and try some gripe water). If your sink is full of dirty dishes . . . surrender! Breathe and know everything will be okay. If you are reading this before your baby joins you, it's a great time to think about what surrendering means to you and your partner. How can you support each other when so much is unknown? Starting to open up the dialogue before this lil' bundle of joy arrives will really help when you are both in the trenches and don't know day from night. Let's dive in.

WTF IS GOING ON?

• • • •

Okay, you probably just watched a tiny human come out of your body. Now you are a mom and expected to keep this little cutie alive. What? Feel free to panic, and then you must press your surrender button.

Even though I literally saw my kids being birthed from my body, I still can't believe I did it. I can't believe I have two kids. I also can't believe I'm finally a mom. It's something I dreamed about for years. When the moment arrived, I happily said, "Okay, now WTF do I do?!" I've talked to many moms over the years, and this feeling is apparently normal. So, enjoy your WTF moment. Embrace it. "The miracle of life" is just that. It's miraculous and bizarre, and it's okay that you don't know the new *you* in this mom bod. Don't think too much, because frankly, you won't have time to! Just breathe and try to enjoy these first moments. It all really does go by so quickly, so try to enjoy each moment. It might not feel like it at the time, but each little phase is so fleeting.

MOM LABELS

• • • •

During these early days and months, it's especially hard to feel like yourself because everything you are doing is new. Every day you are learning about yourself and your baby. And while you may not even realize it, the labels and pressure to *be* some type of mom are there. Often I found that the pressure was only in my head based on my own expectations of how I would be during those first few months. But I also got these expectations from "norms"–other mom friends, family, social media, TV, and more.

Looking back, I don't know why I thought to even have any expectations when there are so many unknowns. Right after my second son was born, I had a weird, itchy rash all over my belly. Every doctor told me to ride it out, that it was just a hormonal reaction. The chill mama I thought I would be (since I was with my first) was thrown out the door–instead I was cranky, tearful, and itchy for the first week. I kept thinking, *I shouldn't be cranky right now. I should be enjoying these first moments.* And there it was—a case of the "shoulds"! I had already labeled myself without even knowing it. In mommyhood, labels just lead to guilt, shame, and disappointment.

YOUR BABY IS ONE OF A KIND, AND SO ARE YOU.

So as you enter this period, maybe you are feeling comfortable with your momness (who are you?). Maybe you aren't sure what the heck you're doing most of the time, which often happens to most of us. Either way, the best bet is to just be yourself and own the kind of new mom you are and accept that every day is different. There is no expectation that you suddenly fit some kind of label. You can be the Village Mom; the Research-Everything Mom; the Badass, No-B.S. Mom; the Must-Prepare-for-Everything Mom; the Blissed-Out-Oh-So-Zen Mom; the

Confident, Happy Mom. Heck, you'll probably be *all* of these moms at some point! Maybe even all on the same day. And that is absolutely okay. Don't worry about perfection. It doesn't exist when it comes to taking care of a newborn. Just do your best to be loving, patient, and kind with yourself and your baby.

Personally, I identified with all these mom labels during the fourth trimester. And some days, I still do! I remember times when I wanted to talk to friends and ask questions and take all of their advice. But other times, I just wanted to figure things out on my own and go with my natural mommy gut instincts. I liked the freedom to be able to say to someone, "Umm, that didn't work with my baby!" and not instantly feel like I was the worst mom on the planet. Your baby is one of a kind, and so are you. You get to navigate this journey in the way that feels most comfortable to you. Whatever that means to you today—just own it, embrace it, and surrender.

#ThisChangedMyMomLife

During the fourth trimester, I started thinking about situations and feelings as though they were bite size. I have taken the phrase "one day at a time" down to "one hour at a time," and remind myself that feelings change and moments and phases are tiny in the big picture. Mommyhood and #adulting, baby . . . This is the craziest ride you've ever been on. But it is all so worth it; I promise.

THE JUGGLE

• • • •

Balance . . . What is that again? I'm sure you're feeling like the day when you can balance time for yourself and time with your sweet lil' bambino is light-years away. But by the end of this fourth trimester, you hopefully are finding a little more time to yourself. Time to breathe, to shower, and, heck, maybe even rest. Maybe you're able to let someone watch the baby while you run to the store all by your awesome self? Sure, it might not feel the same as your pre-kid existence, but that's okay. Your whole life as you've known it has *totally* changed. Instead of that "me time" lasting a whole day, you might only be able to carve out a few minutes here and there. Balancing and prioritizing yourself and your needs as well as your baby's ain't easy. But carving out five to ten minutes in your day to just be by yourself will do wonders for you. That time, however you can get it and whatever you choose to do with it, will really help.

I HAVE TAKEN THE PHRASE "ONE DAY AT A TIME" DOWN TO "ONE HOUR AT A TIME."

Because I had kids when I was older, my mom friends told me to "really enjoy your alone time and ability to work, play, and chill" because with kids, it doesn't happen. They told me that it wasn't just physically hard to chill anymore (cue the screaming kids!), but emotionally hard to relax. How can you relax when you feel so torn, like there is always something else you should be doing for your children instead of yourself? All of their wonderful warnings gave me the mindset of "Yikes, will I be living in this constant zone of no balance now?"

I make it a point each day to give myself even just ten minutes of quiet and being by myself to just breathe. That helps me so much. It's like a little reset all of us moms need in our day. Gosh, even something simple makes a difference. For example, after I buckle my kids into their car seats and close the door, I take my time to walk around the car slowly and breathe a moment! Get those minutes however and wherever you can, right? Remember, recharging is not only great for you but great for your lil' one too. Here's a helpful list of five-to-fifteen-minute break ideas that you can work into your day, all ready for when the moment (hopefully) comes. Breathe, surrender, and try to enjoy any precious minutes of freedom you can get.

Finding Five to Fifteen Minutes of Bliss

- ✧ Have your partner/trusted friend be on baby duty while you go out for a quick walk and breathe in some fresh air.

- ✧ Sit in a quiet place for a cup of tea or coffee and grab a journal or magazine.

- ✧ Light a candle and have a nice hot bubble bath. Soak and relax as long as you can.

- ✧ Watch a TV show that makes you laugh.

- ✧ Do a video call with a good friend.

- ✧ Take a companion to the grocery store and ask for ten minutes to cruise aisles all by yourself, while they watch the baby.

- ✧ Book a postnatal massage for next month.

MAMA NEEDS SLEEP!

• • • •

You probably feel like you're running on fumes at the moment with the only thing fueling you being baby cuddles and cold coffee. You are likely dipping into the ol' energy reserves you never knew you had. The sleep situation is different for everyone and can be the hardest part of this phase. Sleep deprivation is a real thing and can affect you deeply. Your baby's feeding schedules will vary, and your ability to rest may be challenged. But it really is imperative to not just your health and energy, but your baby's, too, so rest whenever and however you can. Try to find comfort in knowing that this phase won't last forever. You've got this! Now . . . go lie down.

I'll admit that some of the best sleep of my life happened between middle-of-the-night feedings. I think it was the simplicity of the nights that allowed me to truly rest between feedings. I was fully focused on feeding the baby and nurturing myself with sleep. I was exhausted but also relaxed in a way that I hadn't experienced before.

During all these sleepless nights, it's hard to believe that you

SLEEP DEPRIVATION—THE STRUGGLE IS REAL!

The reality is new moms, especially during the first few months, are not likely to get long stretches of sleep due to frequent feedings required for newborn babies. Many of us, including me, have experienced new-mom sleep deprivation. But what does it exactly mean? Generally, as adults, we benefit from about seven hours of sleep per night consecutively. While feedings can interrupt sleep, it is important to try to get consolidated sleep for as many hours as possible. This may mean two- or three-hour blocks of sleep at a time. If a partner or family member is involved in caring for the baby at night, utilizing that person to help with diaper changes and getting the baby back to sleep can be useful to help allow for a full three hours of sleep prior to the next feed. Often we can use pumped breast milk and/or formula that someone other than the mother can [administer] to allow for longer stretches of sleep at night too. This is particularly import-ant when someone is suffering from postpartum depression, as sleep is crucial to improving depression.

While the obvious reason for lack of sleep is the baby, who needs frequent feedings, there are other possible issues that can lead to sleep problems as well. For some women, hormonal changes, which lead to activation and anxiety, can prevent sleep. Postpartum anxiety and depression can also lead to difficulty sleeping even when the baby is sleeping. Often, being in a different place where you cannot hear baby cry (a different room, or at a family member's home) can be useful for a small nap to truly detach from the sound of a crying baby.

—Dr. Raveen Gogia, OB/GYN and mom

will sleep again, but I promise you will. Even a few minutes of good sleep can do miracles. Put someone else in charge if you can. Find a time of day that you feel most relaxed and go for it.

Also, high-five yourself for making it through so many sleepless nights, because, let's face it, we women possess some seriously superhuman powers!

YOUR MOODS

· · · ·

You probably already learned in your younger years that mood and hormones go hand in hand. Even knowing that doesn't discount the way you feel. Considering that your body just birthed a baby, it's no secret that your hormones and mood are probably all over the place. Even if you didn't birth your baby . . . the lack of sleep and all this new mommying will have you feeling these changes too. You may feel like you're on a nonstop roller coaster of emotions. Unfortunately, that is not only normal, but to be expected during this time. Add little to no sleep plus a huge decrease in your hormones, and you have a recipe for feeling anything but your former stable self. This is another time that you have to hit the ol' surrender button, but if you feel like you are outside of healthy and safe bounds, reach out to

#ThisChangedMyMomLife

- Don't overdo it; know when to lie down. It's easy to want to start cleaning or doing a load of laundry when you finally get your baby down, but resting when you can is top priority. Sorry, dirty clothes.

- Be honest with your partner when you need a break and switch baby-watching shifts. A rested mama is a happier, more productive mama for all.

- Find zen. Try to set the most relaxing environment you can when it finally is time for a lil' shut-eye. Lie in a dark room, put on some relaxing music, and turn your phone off or leave it in another room to avoid that mommy blog-scrolling temptation.

- Try not to drink coffee or caffeine after 3:00 p.m.

- Follow a nightly routine similar to your baby's—a warm shower or bath, a calming room, and limited screen time before bed.

- Hand the monitor over to your partner (if you can).

- Invest in a good sleep mask and earplugs.

- If you or your baby aren't able to sleep more than a few hours at a time, consult with a medical professional.

your doctor straightaway! Don't think twice; just do it. It's always best to talk to a doctor to make sure everything you are feeling emotionally at this time is okay or if you need some help.

When I was a teenager, whenever I was in a bad mood or upset, my brother instantly would ask, "What are you, on your period or something?" Grrrr. Now he has a twelve-year-old daughter himself, so joke's on him! Once I became pregnant with my first child, I couldn't help but worry my partner would discount my feelings in the same way. "Oh . . . are you crying/screaming/emotional because you're pregnant?" Or the classic "She's just hormonal because she's pregnant." Thankfully, he didn't do that at all (he knows better, ha ha!), and I realized I was judging myself and trying to justify the many feelings I was having—which we *don't* have to do. It's hard to not overanalyze all the feelings and wide range of emotions you are going through. But try to be kind and patient with yourself and the people around you. It's a bit of a bumpy road with all these emotions and hormones, but soon you will be feeling much more like your pre-baby happy and stable self.

THERE'S NO SUGARCOATING IT: The decrease in progesterone and estrogen that occurs after birth is very abrupt. It is important that this decrease occur in the way that it does to signal to your body that pregnancy is over. Your heart, your lungs, your immune system—your entire body needs to go back to its non-pregnant state, and this is one of the ways your body knows it's time to do so. While we know this hormone change impacts the brain, we know very little about how. The impact on emotions, however, is clear and can be profound.

–**Christine Noa Sterling, board-certified OB/GYN and founder of Sterling Parents LLC, sterlingparents.com**

HELLO, ANXIETY

· · · ·

Ohhhhh, the mama anxiety. It can start during pregnancy, and it ends . . . well, I'm not sure it ever does. You may feel that now that you have your baby at home, there is plenty to worry about.

Some of this new-mom worry and anxiety you may expect, and some you may not. Focus on what you could categorize as predictable and take action to feel more comfortable. Most of this is about your ability to feel more at ease. For example, if you are worried about your baby's movement at night, buy a monitor or movement device that covers everything you want to know (Did they move? What's their heart rate? Temperature?). And once you have those things in place, try to breathe and let go of anxiety. You've done all you can do. Now is the beginning of surrendering the control you think you have but really don't. That old surrender button is calling again! Anxiety is a funny thing; it can just creep up on you in the worst of times. Anxiety is like a rude houseguest that doesn't call ahead. So it's important to have some coping mechanisms in place that you can use if the dreaded anxiety monster comes calling.

One thing that really helped me with my anxiety when I was pregnant was to distinguish "predictable anxiety" from "unexpected anxiety" when possible. I carried this philosophy into the fourth trimester. In many ways when I began to think about what was making me anxious with a newborn, it allowed me to consider what I could do to prepare for or avoid it. This is easier said than done.

One thing that immediately made me anxious was going to visit friends to introduce our little cutie. I worried, *What if he is fussy or won't nap? What if he has a giant blowout all over their furniture?* All of this was totally possible, so I created my on-the-go diaper bag. I had extra clothes for me and the baby, extra ziplock bags, extra swaddles that I could lay down to change him, gripe water, gas relief drops, Tylenol, more than enough diapers, etc. Most of the time I left this *giant* bag in the car, but knowing I was mostly prepared for anything made the unexpected easier to deal with. Whereas when there were those unexpected anxieties, I just had to breathe through them and remind myself to try to worry proportionately to the info I had. And let my partner know that I would need extra support if I was getting stuck in a worry cycle.

NOW IS THE BEGINNING OF SURRENDERING THE CONTROL YOU THINK YOU HAVE BUT REALLY DON'T.

Overall, thinking about anxiety in this way, if anything, helped me to own my anxiety and feel a sense of control while also having my tool kit ready for the unknown. One example of this is the panic attacks I had during childbirth and the difference between when I gave birth to my first child and my second. With my first, it was just before pushing that I suddenly started to panic, my heart rate began to rise, and I started to sweat profusely. The nurse got all flustered and asked if I was okay. I remember saying to her, "Well, no, I'm not okay, my entire life is about to change, and a baby is going to come roaring out of my vagina! This is crazy, and I'm scared." The bewildered nurse then reassured me that panic and anxiety were normal during the birthing process and that what I needed to do . . . was just slow down my breathing and focus. And I did. When I was back on the table and ready to start pushing for the delivery of my second born, I

INTRODUCING YOUR WTF TIMER

Allow yourself to sit in the WTF moment for a set time (aim for ten minutes or less). This can trick your brain and allow you to move on.

told my partner and the nurse, "Okay, now I'm going to have my panic attack. I need my WTF timer: five minutes of quiet and just let me freak out. My heart rate is going to go up and it's fine; I will come back to earth in a few minutes." And I did. I cried and I had the shakes, then took a few deep breaths before I told them I was ready to push. For me, I realized that some anxiety is normal. It helps me realize the weight of things and reassures me of what I can control versus when to surrender. As long as I remember I will get through it, I'm okay.

YOUR BODY

• • • •

Okay, let's talk about all the super weird things and new pains going on with your body that, frankly, no one ever talks about. Depending on the type of birth you had, you might be hurting in all kinds of places more than anyone could have prepared you for. Maybe you had a C-section and still struggle to sit up with any ease. Maybe you are still in an adult diaper and, yep, that is a look that no one can prepare you for! Either way, whatever shape that sweet lil' bod of yours is in now, your body is *strong*! Remember . . . it just *created life*! Yep, you. Your body did that! And no matter what you see when you look in the mirror now, know that what your body just achieved is downright miraculous. Look in the mirror, then look at that gorgeous little baby *you made*. Sure, your body has changed forevermore . . . and when you sneeze from now on, you'll have to cross your legs (oh, the joys of birth!), but what you have created should outweigh all the other things.

Sure, it's hard to feel the *G*'s (gorgeous, grounded, grateful) when you have a baby attached to your teat constantly or are barely able to shower. Before you can feel your stunning self again, you might need to tackle a few things.

Just so you remember how strong your body is, write down five things you are proud that your body did during pregnancy and/or the last few months.

1.

2.

3.

4.

5.

BREASTFEEDING

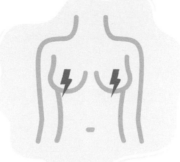

First up, your boobs and nips: if you are breastfeeding, then your precious gals need lots of attention. A light massage before and after feedings can help prevent clogged ducts.

I'm sorry to be the bearer of bad news, but . . . you will most likely get sore, cracked, painful nipples during the first month or two. The good news is you can get ahead with the right tools. And don't worry; though you may shed some tears, it will pass quickly. (I definitely cried.)

So many new mamas I speak with say that the pain they experienced made them give up nursing altogether. Give all these a try and see how your nursing experience improves.

- **Mommy's Bliss Nipple Balm:** You're welcome in advance. This will immediately soothe your nipples and help with healing. It's the perfect combo of soothing coconut oil and healing lanolin. You can use it liberally after each feeding for immediate comfort.
- **Medela Contact Nipple Shields:** Just trust me; buy these immediately! These go on your nipples, and your baby can suck on them and breastfeed, while giving your nips a break. Magical!

- **Lansinoh Soothies:** Yessss, please. Just pop these gel pads in the fridge for instant cooling relief.
- **Lansinoh TheraPearl Breast Therapy Pack:** These are a game changer; use cold from the fridge for calming or use warm if you have any duct blockage.

C-SECTION RECOVERY

- **Mamaway Bamboo Postpartum Belly Band:** This band is super supportive and comfortable.
- **Upspring C-Panty:** This post-C-section recovery underwear helps comfort the wound while also giving your tummy a little compression that can feel supportive.
- **Silicone scar sheets and C-section creams:** Gotta love the innovation and products that, made just for this recovery, both help heal and prevent scarring. The eight-inch-long Frida Mom Silicone Scar Patches are made for this. Motherlove has a C-section cream full of organic and natural ingredients that can help with healing.

DOWN THERE

Nobody mentioned the first poop after birth! OMG. As if the other hole weren't already causing enough drama! Let me explain. Having a bowel movement when your body has just gone through birthing your baby can be very painful. Why? Your stomach and pelvic floor muscles are weakened. You may have developed hemorrhoids, and they may be swollen. Vaginal tearing can extend toward the other hole. Medication can lead to constipation, and you may be dehydrated from breast milk production. But you can prepare.

- **Stool softeners:** You may be sent home with them, or you can find them at any drugstore. Do it!
- **Witch hazel wipes:** These wipes are your new best friends for both areas down there. Pro tip: add a little H. Soothe Cream by Mommy's Bliss to the area before your BM arrives. Whether you have soreness or hemorrhoids, this will surely help. Motherhood, hey? No one said it'd be glamorous.

WHAT THE DISCHARGE?

Umm . . . yeah. For some of us, there is just no end to the new fluids that keep on coming out. Thankfully, there are lots of panty-liner options out there. Always check with your ob-gyn, but there can be various new discharges from birth onward. After birth, you can have postpartum bleeding (with mucus), which is called lochia and can last up to ten days or longer. Delightful, right?

Throughout the fourth trimester and beyond, you may also experience changes with vaginal dryness or other discharge. Always check with your ob-gyn. As mine told me, my cervix was just left a little bit open after birth, so ongoing discharge was normal. All part of that new-mom glow, right?

MY WHAT?

Last and certainly not least is your little friend Ms. Pelvic Floor. Wait. Did you say *pelvic floor*? What? I seriously cannot believe that during pregnancy, neither my ob-gyn nor my friends brought up what my pelvic floor is and how important it is to postpartum recovery and future health "down there." Did you know that *every* woman in France is offered ten to twenty visits with a pelvic-floor physical therapist following every birth she has? You read that correctly . . . This is a real thing! According to l'Assurance Maladie, new moms may be prescribed perineal and abdominal rehabilitation treatments ("la rééducation périnéale") if needed to help heal their pelvic floor and tighten up the goods. Better yet . . . it is all paid for by the French government ("Accouchement et retour à domicile: prise en charge et accompagnement," October 5, 2023). They also serve a cheese course at some French hospitals, so . . . there's that.

The pelvic-floor muscles span the bottom of the pelvis and support the pelvic organs (bladder, bowel, and uterus). It is primarily to help with preventing incontinence (peeing in your pants), but can also help with support of the pelvic organs and sexual pleasure.

Finding Bliss

Listen up, all mamas: Mommy's Bliss has two products made specifically for this time. First up are the Lactation Hydration tablets—these are delicious fizzy tablets you drop in water to help with replenishing vitamins while keeping you hydrated, which helps with milk flow. Next, the Reset My Body gummies are a must-have. Aside from being delicious, these gummies contain biotin, collagen, and vitamin E to support postpartum healing and rejuvenate your hair, skin, and nails. Who doesn't want that?

DON'T GET MAD AT
YOUR BEAUTIFUL BELLY

If your belly still feels bloated and looks big . . . well, yeah, it does; you just had a baby in there stretching you out for nine-plus months. Everyone recovers and has different levels of swelling.

Now is *not* the time to start obsessing over how you look or to focus on weight loss, calorie counting, or eating a restrictive diet. Getting back to your pre-baby sassiness is not a topic for the fourth trimester. Right now, all you need to focus on is eating whole, nourishing foods that will help support your body and the healing process—foods that will help give you the energy you so desperately need, especially if you're breast-feeding. (And if you're craving something, go ahead—eat and enjoy it!)

POST-BABY RECOVERY
TIP: SMOOTHIES

Smoothies, a great source of healing vitamins and nutrition, are easy to sip while you're multitasking. Plus, they're an easy go-to for your partner to help make. Win-win.

These two smoothie recipes are adapted from Jillian Lagasse's.

MAMALICIOUS SMOOTHIE

This smoothie has it all for ultimate postpartum heal-ing: greens to get your body and digestion regulated again; dark cherries and turmeric for anti-inflammation; strawberries for antioxidants; bananas for potassium; flaxseeds for fantastic healthy fats; and oat milk, which is great for breast-milk production. The all-in-one deli-cious smoothie! You'll love this. Yay!

- ❀ 2 large handfuls of organic spinach leaves

- ❀ 1 cup oat milk

- ❀ 1 cup plain Greek yogurt

- ❀ 1 to 2 scoops of your favorite vegan protein powder, as directed on the label. (I like Garden of Life Organic Raw Protein Powder, Vanilla)

- ❀ ½ cup frozen blackberries

- ❀ ½ cup frozen strawberries or raspberries

- ❀ 1 medium banana (frozen is great if you have it)

- ❀ 1 tablespoon ground flaxseeds

- ❀ ½ teaspoon turmeric powder

- ❀ 4 to 5 ice cubes

Place all the ingredients in a large blender. Blend. Add a straw and enjoy!

BREAST-MILK-BOOSTING SMOOTHIE

Drink your way to boosting your breast milk with this delicious smoothie.

Oats are fantastic for helping milk production and are a great source of fiber, which you need now more than ever. This is a complete meal you can blend and drink as you run oat (ha ha . . . dad joke, sorry) the door.

- 1 medium banana (frozen is great if you have it)
- ½ cup frozen mango cubes
- ½ small, ripened avocado
- 1 cup oat milk
- ½ cup almond milk
- ¼ cup oats
- 1 to 2 scoops of your favorite vegan protein powder, as directed on the label
- 1 tablespoon honey
- 1 teaspoon brewer's yeast
- 4 to 5 ice cubes

Place all of the ingredients in a large blender; blend; pour and drink straightaway.

If making smoothies isn't your jam, here are some other foods to consider to support healing and nourishing your body. (Karen Pallarito, "Your Postpartum Nutrition Guide," What to Expect, August 27, 2021, https://www.whattoexpect.com/first-year/post partum/postpartum-diet-nutrition-questions-answered/.)

Satisfying Fats!	Immunity-Boosting Colors!	Milk-Boosting Grains	Happy-Gut Dairy
Lean Beef	Berries	Oats	Cheese
Bone Broth	Fruit	Quinoa	Eggs
Chicken	Cooked Green, Leafy Veggies		Greek Yogurt
Salmon			
Organic Tofu	Carrots		
Coconut Milk			
Almonds			
Provides			
Protein	Vitamins	Fiber	Probiotics
Iron	Minerals	Folate	Vitamin D
Vitamin D	Antioxidants	Iron	Protein
Collagen	Fiber		Calcium
Omega-3 Fatty Acids			Choline

You can also keep taking your prenatal vitamins or start taking postnatal ones.

BREASTFEEDING IS NO JOKE

Growing up, I had always heard my mom talk about breast-feeding because she worked as a lactation consultant and doula. I remember hearing about the technical side of it, something about angles and latching, nipples, breast pumps, and breastfeeding pillows. The "breast is best" mantra was loud, but I think that implied it would be easy, so why wouldn't you breastfeed?

> # IT'S A FRIGGIN' PROJECT THAT CAN BECOME ALL-CONSUMING. IT CAN BE A HEALTHY PROJECT, OR IT CAN BE TOO MUCH AND START TO TAKE AWAY FROM ALL THE BLISS.

After a while, I tuned it out, until there I was with a new baby and ready to put my infant on my boob and breastfeed like a champ. Umm. No. That's not what happened. Suddenly, I became aware of all these real technicalities; it was like trying to build a piece of Ikea furniture where one piece fit and the other didn't, and then the clock was ticking and . . . ahhhhh!

It was like breastfeeding had its own language, an instruction manual with tons of gaps, and there was an alarm clock ticking in my head. WTF! Luckily, my mom was there to help me with learning to adjust and find the right positions. She let me cry when I had cracked nipples and gave me her tips to soothe them. What I didn't expect was the mental and emotional toll that came with breastfeeding. It's a friggin' project that can become all-consuming. It can be a healthy project, or it can be too much and start to take away from all the bliss.

I felt stressed out about staying on top of all the feedings and was constantly checking the time. Sometimes I wanted the hours to be shorter and sometimes longer. I felt confused about how much milk my baby boy was actually getting. Of course, this led to worry and shame that I was defective, not being able to give my baby what he needed. I worried about my right boob versus my left boob—was one better, providing more milk? Why was the left more comfortable for me? I had felt pressure to have my partner bottle feed on occasion so I could take a break. But then I had to pump when he gave him the bottle, so it wasn't really a break! The economics of my milk supply versus demand were so daunting. But I can't deny that when milk was flowing, those moments with my baby were precious. The powerful feeling that came with my ability to feed my baby was unreal, the bond beyond special.

And then it was back to stressful, and slowly guilt and shame barged in. With my second baby, by the second month I wasn't producing enough, so I had to supplement with formula. Which kind of formula? There were questions, worries, and pressures that came along with this that I had never anticipated and that women experience differently. Once again, this means this is your time to do it *your* way.

DID YOU KNOW THIS?

If you're breastfeeding, you need about **sixteen cups of water** per day, according to the Academy of Nutrition and Dietetics.

As a new parent, it's always hard to figure out what is truly best for you *and* your baby *and* your family when it feels like they all conflict. I like how Emily Oster, author of *Cribsheet* and other awesome books, brings data and cost-benefit perspectives to the table to help new parents make decisions.

In a *Freakonomics* interview about whether to breastfeed or not, she summarizes her thoughts on how the decision should come down to "what works" rather than what society expects: "There is an increasing recognition . . . that some of the ways we have been pressuring people to breastfeed have been counter-productive." My takeaway: with so much information out there on all things parenting, using your own cost-benefit analysis may actually help you get to what *your* way is.

The takeaways are the following:

- Relax and do the best you can.
- Think about the cost/benefit of breastfeeding for you. If you are so stressed, what impact is that having on you and your baby?
- Your baby is healthy so far? Try not to worry unless your pediatrician tells you to change course.

YOUR RELATIONSHIP

• • • •

Whatever road your journey to parenthood has taken, be it that you and your partner created this little human yourselves or that you went through adoption or surrogacy, hopefully the miracle of having your baby has you both blissed-out.

It's so important to try to enjoy all these precious (and sleep-deprived) moments together. Try to keep things simple as far as connecting, since your time is very much focused on your lil' one right now. But, oh yeah, your partner exists too! Maybe have a relative babysit during nap time and sneak off for a quick coffee date? Or order takeout from your fave place and eat together after the nightly bed routine . . . and maybe even sneak in thirty minutes of Netflix time? Talk together about the new ways you both want to spend time connecting.

Another biggie is talking honestly about each other's expectations about intimacy. Obviously, you don't want to completely avoid the topic with your partner, but it's hard to be in a place where you even want an intimate connection after what your incredible body has just gone through! You might not be feeling your best, your sexiest . . . That is normal! It can be common for partners to feel a bit left out during this time and for some, even a bit jealous. I know; humans are crazy beings, right? But

GET-AHEAD TIP

If you and your partner have had a vibrant sex life and frequent date nights, chat about expectations ahead of the baby's arrival.

Examples of how to initiate the chat:

♥ "We should probably set our expectations around when we can have sex again and let's make sure to talk about it around six weeks."
♥ "Let's come up with how we can have our first new date night (maybe seventy-five minutes) and we can get excited for it."

try to look at it from your partner's point of view. For the past however long, they've had you and your love, care, and attention fully. Going from all to nothing is hard for anyone. So it's imperative to talk about each other's needs and wants during this time to keep anyone from jumping on the ol' resentment train. Acknowledge that your partner may feel a little left out at times or feel helpless, and find ways to include your partner and reassure them when they are helping. Ask for help and be specific. Apparently, they can't read our minds! Who knew?

I was so blessed that my partner did lots of little things to help and show his love during this time. He always refilled my special big glass of cold water. He did a stealth pillow tuck under my arm during feedings, and he encouraged me to nap and shower while he took on baby-watch duty. He took the initiative to take care of everything home-related, from cleaning to groceries, during the first few months, which was incredibly helpful since my hands were . . . umm . . . very full! Sometimes just having your partner ask what they can do to help can make this "new" partnership even stronger and less stressful. I mean, you are trying to keep a human alive. Who has time to worry about dirty dishes too?

Now it's time to leave this book open to the following pages so that your partner can read your answers. Also let your partner fill out their section to open up a discussion.

FOR YOU:

My partner makes me feel special and loved when ____

_____

_____

_____.

It would be super helpful if my partner _____

_____

_____

_____.

I'm feeling a little insecure about _____

_____

_____

_____.

Ways I'd like to connect with my partner: _____

_____

_____

_____.

Here's where I am with intimacy: _____

_____

_____

_____.

FOR YOUR PARTNER:

Some little things you can do to let me know you still
care: _____

_____

_____

_____

_____

_____.

Ways I'd like to connect with you: _____

_____

_____

_____

_____

_____.

Here's where I am with intimacy: _____

_____

_____

_____

_____

_____.

YOUR VILLAGE

• • • •

It can be hard navigating friendships when a baby is attached to you . . . quite literally!

Who are your village people? You know . . . your core friend gang, your ride-or-dies, your there-anytime-and-all-times. Your village comprises the few friends whom you know you can rely on any time of the day or night and are your judgment-free safe zone. Let's face it: you need them right now more than ever. During this time, it's so important to try to find the energy to connect with them. Even if it's just a quick hey, you'll be thankful you did.

You may also start building your new village right away, if your hospital offers new-mom groups. Nothing like another mom going through the same phases as you to understand the middle-of-the-night feedings and so much more. While everything is new in the fourth trimester, it can be a time when you truly connect and bond with other new moms.

However you do it, rely on your village peeps, because most of them, new or old, can offer some comfort and advice or at least deliver you Starbucks! You might not be feeling up to getting all dolled up right now to go out in the world to hang with

them in person, and that is okay! Thank goodness for text mes-saging and a million connection apps if you'd rather stay home in your sweats to connect with them. In whatever way you feel like connecting with your core group, be sure to keep it up for your own mental well-being. Think of your three closest friends and keep them in the loop as much as you can. Don't worry about other people you feel obliged to invite over. Now is *your* time, and it's precious. You can certainly spread out the line of visitors over a few months. Depending on where some of your friends are at in their adulting journey, they may or may not un-derstand the new stress you are under.

Setting boundaries and expectations (#adulting) ahead of your little one joining the party can be a good idea too. It will help everyone if you are clear and up-front about what kind of support you need from your crew. Sometimes mothering, es-pecially in this early phase, can feel terribly lonely and isolating. It helps so much to know you are *not* alone and you have an amazing support system to help you. It will make such a differ-ence. Maybe try meeting up for a coffee date or ask one of your besties to join you for a walk in the park to breathe some much-needed fresh air. Going out for a four-hour dinner is probably not what you want right now! Try to verbalize what works for *you* . . . because right now, that's the way it has to be. You and your baby's schedule take priority. Your mom friends will get it. For nonparents, just keep things simple and expectations low.

NOW IS *YOUR* TIME, AND IT'S PRECIOUS.

For me during this phase, I quickly realized that phone calls required too much energy, so texting was how I could best con-nect. One of the best pieces of advice I received was about

THE FRIEND WHO GOT AWAY

You know, the one that suddenly goes MIA when the baby is born? It happens. Be mindful that some friends have their own stuff that may come into play when you have a baby. It isn't about you; it's about them and something they are going through that is sensitive. Being patient with them can go a long way if they aren't ready to connect.

setting clear expectations for visitors during those first few weeks. I would tell them that forty-five minutes was about my max hangout time, and I'd limit it to only one visitor per day. My partner was a huge support and often helped to make the (sometimes) awkward suggestion of "Hey, babe, don't you need to nap because it's only forty-five minutes until the next feeding?" or something like that to signal time was up. You and your partner need a safe word or phrase. This was our cue to try to get people out the door without being rude—like, "Thanks for the baby gift and casserole, but you gotta *go*!"

At first, I feared people would walk away, feeling like I was being too rude or unkind. But I learned that most people appreciated the clarity of knowing what my time limits were. Most people are happy to respect your boundaries once they know what they are, and, no, mind reading doesn't count. Let's face it: all they really want is to see your cute baby, get some sniffs on that sweet lil' baby hair, and get a few yummy baby cuddles! Who doesn't want that, right? It's hard to blame people for wanting to overstay their welcome when the gorgeous gift of a baby is there to enjoy. Stick to putting in the effort to maintain your village people, even when you are feeling utterly exhausted. It really will help. And remember: you've got this!

Being a new mom is a fulfilling, often tiring, and magical journey. Unfortunately, though, there is no instruction manual for this adventure. You're going to need support in a lot of ways . . . in fact, *all* the ways! While every mom's journey is unique, you can benefit a lot by listening to other moms' experiences. Sometimes just knowing someone else out there has gone through what you're going through in this new-mama adventure can really help to make it feel more manageable and to give you hope. This help can come in many different forms. Perhaps just physically being in the company of other new moms can really feel comforting and reassuring, like a Mommy & Me class or the local park. Look up new-mom groups in your local area that meet in person (usually free and offered through hospitals, community centers, and churches). That might be exactly the type of support you need.

Maybe the logistics of a group are too stressful, or you're an introvert who can't take the energy of other moms right now. Maybe you feel more comfortable getting support online instead of face to face. Luckily, support can be found in many

#ThisChangedMyMomLife

I'm not sure why it was hard for me to accept that my smartphone was my lifeline to, well, everything. But once I did, boy, did I embrace it. It made so many things more convenient and less stressful. So . . . say hello to your new bestie! Here are some great suggestions for support in different ways:

Emotional Support

- **Betterhelp.com.** They offer fantastic online therapy services.
- **Ginger.com.** They offer online emotional and mental health support.
- **Hellolunajoy.com.** They offer holistic online therapy services for moms.

Childcare Support

- **Sittercity.com.** They offer babysitting, nannies, and tutors that have varied experience.
- **Care.com.** This is one of the OG's for finding solid childcare in your area whether you need a sitter for a date night or someone on a more permanent basis. Now you can add home help to your request too.
- **Babysitters4Hire.** They've been around for more than twenty years and offer childcare options and helpful tools like sample interview questions you should ask before hiring someone.

Housekeeping Support

☼ **Nextdoor.com.** This helpful platform connects you and your neighbors and allows you to chat in a forum to ask questions, get recommendations, and even sell things.

☼ **Tidy.com.** This is one of the quickest ways to book top-rated cleaners in your area.

Other Support

☼ **Instacart.** This app is easy to use and gets groceries delivered within a few hours.

☼ **Gobble.com.** This meal-kit delivery company was voted #1 by *Parents* magazine, probably based on the convenience and yummy recipes. Their chefs do all the prep for you to make a homemade dinner in fifteen minutes or less.

☼ **FamilyWall.com.** This offers a shared calendar, grocery lists, and to-do lists.

☼ **Marco Polo.** This app allows you to video share with friends or groups of friends. They can see you and your cute babe without all the coordinating of video calls.

☼ **Relish.** This app helps you stay connected to your partner during the ups and downs of this new chapter.

ways thanks to technology, social media, and much more that have changed the way we live and support each other. There are so many fantastic online mommy-support groups, chats, apps, and forums to dive into.

Think of what suits you in this moment and choose that. Let go of all the "shoulds." You don't have to be that mom who goes to all the mom-and-baby groups. Or the one who feels too scared to reach out. Supermom isn't actually real or something to strive toward becoming—it's just you being you. Practice and prioritize what feels authentic for you (let the apps and your community do the rest!).

I have also had many conversations with friends who felt that their parents or in-laws were judging them because of the super expensive monitor they bought or because they had an app that tracked the baby's feeding and pooping. While I also have joked about my parents judging me, it isn't really their fault. Our environment and worries are incredibly different from when our parents raised us, leading to differences in perspectives on how to parent, what tools are important, etc. For some, this leads to wonderful conversations and support. For others, it leads to defensiveness and feeling judged. Take a minute to think about how you want to engage with and react to these kinds of new conversations. And remember: they didn't get an instruction manual on how to be grandparents, just as you didn't get one on how to be a parent.

It's also helpful to talk with family about visiting, childcare expectations, and desires *before* the baby is born. Nothing like assuming Grandma is going to watch the baby five days a week, only to find out they are only comfortable with one afternoon for two hours. Another factor is that nobody has met *your* baby yet and met you as a new mom. Needs and care may change often, so remind them of this. Everything is fluid in the fourth trimester. The more flexible your support is, the better.

GRANDPARENTS: AWESOME OR TOTALLY *NOT* AWESOME?

When my first son, Julian, was born, the vision I had for family gatherings and grandparents' help was very different from the reality. I was the last one of my siblings to have kids and was almost forty. This also meant my parents were older than I had thought they would be as grandparents to my children. It was hard for me to accept that watching a young baby requires a lot of attention and patience, which was just too much for my parents. As much as I didn't expect this reality, I had to accept it quickly and make sure I had consistent childcare in place instead of always counting on the grandparents to do the job. In a lot of ways, this worked out for the best, as we usually ended up spending time all together with my kids when they were babies and saved "babysitting" for a real babysitter. It seemed to be a much more enjoyable situation for everyone.

FOUR THINGS TO DISCUSS WITH GRANDPARENTS BEFORE THE BABY ARRIVES

1. **Visiting expectations immediately after the baby is born:** Set your desires first. Make sure to address when you feel comfortable with visitors, using specifics (within hours to after a few days or weeks) and how long they can plan to visit (thirty minutes versus the whole day). Share what you think may be a way for them to be helpful, from preparing a meal to doing some laundry.

2. **Their vision:** Ask them how they feel about being grandparents. What do they envision for their role? Are they down for full-on blowouts and barf, or just light baby watching here and there?

3. **Childcare expectations:** Are you and they clear and in agreement on expectations of involvement? You can say, "I am so excited for you to spend time with the baby. I'm also figuring out childcare soon. What are your thoughts on when and how you want to help and visit? Should we set something up regularly, or should we just stick with spontaneity?"

4. **Parenting styles and advice:** Are you ready for unsolicited advice? You can say, "I am so grateful for any tips you have! I also want to learn things on my own." Or, "I am so excited to be a mom, and I really want to figure things out on my own. I will reach out for help and advice when I need it."

MONEY STUFF

• • • •

Time to prioritize where your dollars are going!

It probably comes as no shock to you that babies cost us money. Like . . . a lot of money. You may have had to spend money to have or adopt a baby. And now that the baby is here, there is *so* much stuff being thrown at you to buy. Especially at 3:00 a.m. when you are awake doing the night feed and scrolling on Instagram.

During the fourth trimester, my desire was to be as comfy as possible and for things to be as convenient as they could be while I was recovering and sleep deprived (adios to extra stress). I spent money on things that seemed like they were going to be truly helpful and last more than a minute.

TEN MUST-HAVES
(THAT AREN'T COMMON!)

1. Armrest organizer—all your essentials conveniently next to you during feedings and naps.
2. Big cup with straw—it's amazing how thirsty you can get.
3. Doorknob cushion—because some people don't close doors quietly.
4. Family Wall app—a shared app that has grocery lists and a calendar.
5. Comfortable earplugs—not the crappy foamy ones, but ones that work and feel good.
6. A good-quality eye mask.
7. Back-seat blowout kit—box in the car with garbage bag, wipes, extra baby clothes, extra mom shirt, Mommy's Bliss gas drops and gripe water, and Tylenol.
8. Blackout curtains for the baby's room and yours!

9. Portable phone charger.
10. A travel/portable monitor—makes traveling easier and more relaxing.

YOUR IDENTITY

• • • •

Did you know you are raising yourself too?

Sometimes becoming a parent triggers feelings in us that we didn't know were there or sad memories that have been pushed deep down inside since our own childhood. Say what now? Yep. This may be true for you or your partner. Of course, it may depend on what kind of upbringing and parenting either of you had. Having honest conversations is important so that both of you are aware of historical family baggage that can come into play when you least expect it. These conversations also allow you to call it out and look for support to break those nasty negative cycles. It may make you or your partner nervous to dive in, but whenever you can, it will be worth it. And you might not know it's an issue until it is, and then it's crucial to address it.

Unfortunately, having kids can trigger us in unexpected ways, especially when your children are the same age at which

THE YUCKY STUFF THAT YOU MUST ADDRESS

- ◆ Childhood abuse (physical, sexual, emotional)
- ◆ Childhood trauma
- ◆ Death or loss of family members
- ◆ Household dysfunction (such as mental health, divorce, or substance use)

you or your partner may have experienced trauma. It's crucial to face this as honestly and therapeutically as possible.

My partner and I had very different childhoods, but we aligned on what kind of parents we wanted to be. We aligned on the qualities we wanted to emulate from our parents and those we wanted to avoid to try to break a negative cycle.

Here are the three topics we talked about to get to a place of empowerment around the way our childhood baggage could impact our parenting. Use this also as a prompt for you to reflect on your own experience.

PARENTING STYLES:

How did my parents parent me? _____
_____
_____
_____
_____.

I remember I loved it when my parent(s) _____
_____
_____
_____
_____.

I remember the hard moments with my parents were
usually related to _____
_____
_____
_____
_____.

A few things I don't want to do that my parent(s) did are
_____
_____
_____
_____.

CHILDHOOD TRAUMA AND CHALLENGES:

If I had trauma or very adverse circumstances, how have I processed these experiences? _____

_____

_____

_____

_____

_____.

I think I could be triggered by my own kids in these ways:

_____

_____

_____

_____

_____.

EMOTIONS:

How were emotions expressed between parents and kids in my childhood home? _____

_____

_____

_____

_____

_____

_____.

How was I or wasn't I encouraged to share my feelings as a kid? _____

_____

_____

_____

_____

_____

_____.

Was there more talking or yelling growing up? _____

_____

_____

_____

_____

_____

_____.

How will I/we model the emotional intelligence and communication skills we want for our kids? _____

_____

_____

_____

_____

_____

_____.

In a lot of ways, you also give birth to a new you and are raising yourself not only to be a mom, but to be the best version of yourself for you and your baby. This is not easy! From my six years' experience of being a mom, I had no idea that I would also be learning so much about myself. Kids are like a mirror, and sometimes we don't always love what is seen in that reflection. Not to mention all the "OMG . . . I am acting just like *my* mom" moments you'll probably experience, which can be a good or a bad thing! If you had a challenging childhood or suffered trauma in the past, finding a great therapist can do wonders not only for you, but for your children and your partnership too.

MOM GUILT

. . . .

Ahhh . . . the mom guilt. Mom guilt is *such* a crazy thing that seems to just become a part of us when we become new moms. And I hate to break this news to you if you don't already know it, but it doesn't ever really go away. We just learn to quiet that little monster down. Save it for the actual moments of real guilt.

So, what is this mom guilt I speak of?

Here's my definition:

> **mom guilt**
> *the feeling or worry that you should be doing more*
> *or that you are not a good enough mom; a feeling*
> *of guilt when a mom does something for herself*

During these first few months, the most guilt I felt was associated with breastfeeding. I felt bad that I wasn't making enough milk, and I felt guilty about supplementing with formula. Not to mention, my mom was a lactation consultant, so I felt additional

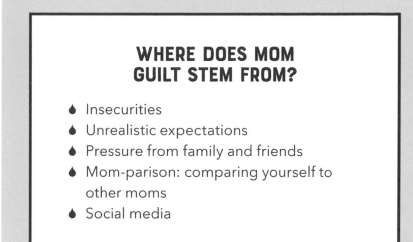

WHERE DOES MOM GUILT STEM FROM?

◆ Insecurities
◆ Unrealistic expectations
◆ Pressure from family and friends
◆ Mom-parison: comparing yourself to other moms
◆ Social media

pressure to breastfeed like a goddess. (Yeah. Friggin'. Right!) But looking back now, I realize my baby was *so* healthy and happy. Did I really need to waste so much of my energy on feeling guilty?

We need to lose the mom guilt especially when it comes to feeding our babies formula if need be. We all as moms are just trying to do our best and raise healthy and happy lil' ones. Sometimes we can't produce enough milk to do that on our own. There are choices we have to make, and sometimes that help might just come in powdered form. And that's totally okay! As long as it's reducing your stress and helping your baby grow healthfully, let go of any preconceived ideas that breast milk is the only way. Sure, breast is best . . . We all know that! It's drilled into us a million times at every pre- and postnatal appointment. But what if you can't breastfeed? Luckily, times, technology, science, and formulas have all changed alongside many evolving cultural norms. If your pediatrician feels your baby is healthy, then continue doing what you think is best for you and the baby.

I HAVE FOUND THAT MOM GUILT TENDS TO SURFACE when a mother feels incapable of doing something that is deemed "natural" for other mothers. Even in my own experience, the pregnancy and birth journey was not what I expected. I have seen moms experience this guilt when they feel responsible for an outcome that did not go as planned, more specifically, with birth trauma, infertility issues, and IVF pregnancy. Mothers don't intend to face challenges when it comes to conception and delivery, so, when that becomes the experience, some moms may internalize these feelings, blaming themselves for their inability to conceive and deliver their babies as one would "typically" be able to do. It is important to recognize how valid these feelings are, acknowledge them as they present, and appropriately process them so they don't have a significant impact on your mental health. I am grateful to play the role I have in helping new moms work through these tough emotions, so know that you aren't alone and there are professional resources that can support you. Remember, guilt is a typical response to these events, and it has no impact on how wildly capable and amazing you will be as a mother.

—Nicole Kumi, PhD, PMH-C, and
CEO of The Whole Mom, thewholemom.com

Whichever way you end up feeding your baby, let go of guilt, and embrace *your way*. Then move forward with peace and love, baby. You'll have plenty of time to have the ol' mom guilt tripping you up within the months and years to come! You don't need to get a head start on it now. And to be sure you don't get stuck in mom guilt, here is your first permission slip. Trust me; you will need to keep this close.

PERMISSION SLIP

FOR THIS MOM
TO LET THAT SH*T GO

I, Yasmin Kaderali, hereby grant permission for you, _____, to release all mom guilt, shame, and judgment effective immediately. ***Let that sh*t go.***

Remember, you are doing your best. Some days your best is crap, and that's really okay. Stop comparing yourself to other moms online. You are finding **your own way** as a mom.

Furthermore, I grant you permission to ignore all hostility, bad vibes, and unsolicited advice from others, and to **CELEBRATE** yourself as the brilliant, **BADASS MAMA-GODDESS** that you are.

SIGNED: _____ *Y. Kaderali* _____

This permission slip is valid in all locations and at all times, including and especially at your in-laws', in the event of a blowout diaper, and after a sleepless night, week, or year.

WHERE IS THE BLISS?

• • • •

Don't you just love it when you're scrolling Instagram and you see all these new moms who are super-blissed-out, while you feel like a total mess still wearing a giant pad, with dark circles under your eyes? Just like Instagram is full of moments (literally), so is your life. And while being a new mom is super hard, it hopefully comes with a side of blissful moments with your new babe. I remember those first moments of eye contact and how much it filled me up. But while I did have those moments with my new cutie-pie, I found a lot of bliss in the relief of not being pregnant anymore, because it was a challenging and anxious nine months. Relief in making it through childbirth, which I had so much fear about. Amazed at my strength to get through sleepless nights. So remember when scrolling, moments can be fabulous and beautiful, and one second later messy and frustrating, and maybe that's the bliss—that we can hold all of it and know it's all true.

CHECKING IN ON YOURSELF

• • • •

While some people call this self-care, I think we have to know how we want to take care of ourselves, and what parts of us need taking care of. We immediately think self-care means a massage or going for a walk alone, and while it certainly can, it is really about finding the time to check in on yourself and knowing how to nurture yourself. Especially during this phase, you are healing and taking it easy—no need to try for a power yoga class!

I like to think about my self-care and self check-in this way: my heart and mind, and my body and health. While these parts of myself are all so connected, I find that separating them out while I'm in a reflective mode helps me see the areas I need to work on more clearly. I started this in the fourth trimester and still use this tool today.

I've included Heart and Mind and Body and Health checklists for three separate phases. The focus of these checks—and therefore the questions and actions on each list—may vary at different phases, so there are slight variations based on what you may be needing.

MY HEART AND MIND

THOUGHTS

- ○ Am I feeling present?
- ○ Am I feeling pressure to be a certain way?
- ○ Do I have enough moments of calm?
- ○ Am I okay being patient with myself? With this phase?
- ○ Am I coping with the unpredictable flow of things right now?

ACTIONS

- 👍 Talk to a friend, therapist, or partner.
- 👍 Leave gratitude reminders (ask my partner to as well).
- 👍 Find time alone to think *and* not think.
- 👍 Seek laughter and lightness.

MY BODY AND HEALTH

THOUGHTS

O Am I being patient and gentle with my body's healing process?

O Am I feeling grateful for my body's strength and what it went through?

O Do I trust my body?

O Am I having positive or negative self-talk about my body?

ACTIONS

👍 Eat healthy.

👍 Enjoy food.

👍 Move my body.

👍 Get sunshine; go outside.

DIFFICULT PREGNANCY, BIRTH TRAUMA, IVF, AND OTHER CIRCUMSTANCES

While you may be so grateful for your precious baby, it may have been a challenging road to get to this place. It's hard to imagine having coexisting feelings of gratitude and sadness, anger, confusion, and guilt. As much as we plan for and envision all of the pathways leading to being a mom, in reality it may have been very different, and it can take time to process the trauma or effects it is still having on your life.

I've heard from friends that had to do rounds of IVF that once they were happily pregnant and had any feelings of disappointment (triggered perhaps by learning the baby's gender), the disappointment immediately turned to shame. They felt like they weren't supposed to feel upset or disappointed because they should have been incredibly grateful for the pregnancy. They also feared being judged for not being completely happy. So if this is a voice you are hearing in your head, talk to a therapist about it. You're not alone, and you can get through this.

#ThisChangedMyMomLife

I haven't told many people this, but during my pregnancies, I had to give myself a shot in the stomach area twice a day, every f*cking day of being pregnant and six weeks after giving birth. I cried when my ob-gyn told me. She said due to something in my medical history, this was important to keep me and the baby safe. There was no argument, just anger and fear. I started to do the shots, and I hated it. My husband would hear me crying in the bathroom twice a day for the first few months. I can't say that I got used to it, but the routine became the norm. Then the anxiety about having to do this all over again if we had a second baby was daunting. It was hard to talk to anyone about this, especially in my older age group, because I felt that I should just be grateful to be pregnant. During my second pregnancy, I did tell a friend about this and she said, "Damn, Yaz, you're a badass." I had never thought about it that way.

But now, looking back, I do think I was a total badass! Over five hundred self-administered shots to get here and I did it. It taught me to own my feelings and take time to be in them without shame, and then reframe the self-talk when it feels right.

CHAPTER 2

THE FIFTH TRIMESTER

Baby: From four to six months
You: Still tired, less sore, and feeling a little more like yourself

By now, you've mastered swaddling your baby like a little burrito and you're accustomed to plans being detoured by diaper blowouts and barfy shirts. A lovely bonus is that the smiles and cooing have arrived in this phase, which are hopefully filling your heart up and making all the sleepless nights worth it. But life is still not without the unexpected bumps, sleep regressions, and not knowing that there are different nipple flow sizes (oops!). There is still plenty to learn about yourself and your little cutie-pie. Hopefully you feel more like you have found your groove and have established somewhat of a routine. The other nice part about this phase is there is a little more room for *you*. This may mean more sleep, some time alone without the baby, and a little more head space to process this new life.

WTF IS GOING ON?

• • • •

You've managed to keep your sweet baby (and yourself) alive for a few months. Congrats! Maybe you feel like you're in the groove of mommying, or maybe not. Imposter syndrome is real. This whole mommying thing might not feel natural or comfortable at all, and that's okay. You might think the mom across the street seems *so* together with her designer diaper bag and not one hair of her perfect blowout out of place. Who the f*ck cares!

COMPARISON
IS THE THIEF
OF **JOY**

—TEDDY ROOSEVELT

Everyone is different, and every mom moms in a different way. All that matters is how you feel while surviving these phases and that you and your baby are as happy and healthy as can be. Literally, that is it. I'm sure you're learning that parenting is

Finding Bliss

Try to think of activities you could do every day at the same time to break up the naps and feedings that would make the day feel somewhat predictable for you. Ideas could include:

- ✧ A morning walk and coffee-shop run
- ✧ Baby and mommy nap time
- ✧ A walk to a local park
- ✧ A Mommy & Me playgroup
- ✧ Afternoon music time
- ✧ Yoga mat and tickle time

moment by moment, hour by hour, day by day, feed by feed. You and your baby will ebb and flow, and right now your schedule has to be flexible. The question is, can you enjoy this go-with-the-flow time? Are you able to find a sense of control amid so much that is out of your control? Setting a routine for even just one or two things a day can really help you and your baby have some peace and structure with knowing what is to come. But, of course, be prepared for things to come up last minute and the need to be flexible and adaptable. You know with lil' ones, things happen all the time, be it teething, sickness, bad sleep, and so on. Adapt to life as it happens. Trust me; that is the only way to get through it!

The bedtime routine was our staple, and if you haven't already established a routine, the fifth trimester is a great time to start. Achieving consistency with that routine made my family feel like we could predict at least one part of the day. It also became "family time" when my partner joined in. When we were all together, I didn't feel that things were reliant solely on me, which really helped my own sanity.

As much as I've always thought that routines are stressful and limiting, it surprised me during the first year how much I needed and enjoyed consistency. Predictability is something we humans, big and small, need.

MOM LABELS

• • • •

The past few months can probably best be described as a complete blur. Some days you feel like a natural mom (whatever that means), and other days it feels like you are stuck in that dream where you are at a new job, maybe naked, with no idea what you are supposed to be doing. The path you're on doesn't come with a map, and as much as you might want one, once you get where you're going, you'll be glad you made your own way. The confidence you will get from trying, testing, failing, and doing all that again is worth it. The gut instinct you may suddenly feel when you're like, "Umm . . . no, we did it this way because it worked" will reassure you that you are a badass mom!

Even though it's only been a short time since bringing this new baby (and new you) into the world, you have actually already started your "mom skills" résumé. What new skills would you add? Don't catch a case of the "shoulds" or labels or other-mom-comparing. That's not what matters. Give yourself permission to be satisfied with exactly where you are right now.

Now, take a deep breath and remember tomorrow is a new day. What's a short mantra that resonates with you for this week?

MAMA IZABOSS

BADASS MOM

CONTACT

☎ 123-456-7890; text, don't call

✉ thiscoolmama@gmail.com

📍 123 Anywhere St.,
Any City, Any State

SKILLS

Inventory Management

Procurement

Event Planning & Facilitation

Conflict Resolution

Time Management

Project Management

Multitasking Across
Departments

Tech Support

Customer Service

Analytics & Psychoanalysis

Healthcare

EDUCATION

CrazyCarefree High School
1991–1995

When I Had Fun University
1996–2001

OBJECTIVE

Badass Mom seeks a role where she can leverage multitasking and emotional management across the marketing, sales, finance, operations, HR, and basically all departments of the organization.

Ideal company will allow her to maintain high stress levels, lack of time to herself, and the constant addition of more to her plate.

Role must allow for napping and day drinking. And in-office vacation where nobody knows she is on vacation.

EXPERIENCE

CEO OF HUMAN SUSTAINABILITY & SURVIVAL
Home
2016–Present

- Led a nine-month incubation product resulting in human life.
- Delivered tiny human in perfect health.
- Maintained all human life in the household while under significant stress.
- Increased household happiness and purpose factor by 350 percent.
- Led multiple projects for stakeholders, achieving never-before-seen results.

COO OF EVERYTHING
Home
2010–2014

- Grew family by 133 percent in Year 1.
- Managed all inventory, procurement, and planning for the organization.
- Led annual strategy for everything.
- Sustained human life and optimal health across stakeholders.
- Stayed on budget for all projects.

Share it with your partner or one of your village people and ask them to remind you of it if you're feeling a bit rough or hopeless.

My mantra during the first six months was mostly about reassuring myself that I had the inner strength to get through the many challenges and unknowns. I would tell myself, *Just be you and everything will be all right.* I know it sounds cheesy, but this has been my professional mantra too. I have confidence and faith that by being my true self, which does feel fairly well rounded, things will work out okay. More importantly, I feel true to myself. Even when I had no idea what I was doing as a mom, just knowing that I was doing it my way and following my natural gut instincts really helped.

THE JUGGLE

· · · ·

The reality of meeting all the new needs of your baby, your home, yourself, and your partner can feel . . . well, truly overwhelming. Is there a balancing act? For me, having a daily list is key to making things happen. When your baby is four to six months old, the list is going to be short, but that's okay; it can help to set expectations for your day. Any successes, no matter how big or small, will give you a feeling of accomplishment.

During the fifth trimester, I tried to get in three mini wins. Some days, I would do all three (go me!); other days, things would of course pop up, and I might not get to any of them. Think of a few things you'd like to accomplish each day. Even if you get only one in, these are the things *you* need to feel human again! Everyone's ideas of what a mini win is will look different. The biggest thing to remember in this new parenting journey is that you have to be able to go with the flow and adapt. If you don't get any of your mini wins done, it's okay! Tomorrow is a new day, baby . . . Just keep on going.

MY MANTRA TODAY IS:

**SUPERMOM ISN'T
ACTUALLY REAL OR
SOMETHING TO STRIVE
TOWARD BECOMING—IT'S
JUST YOU BEING YOU.**

Finding Bliss

My mini wins—yes, it is possible to feel productive with these!

- ✥ Take a quiet shower.
- ✥ Nap.
- ✥ Get outside.
- ✥ Eat a slow-paced meal.
- ✥ Stretch my body.

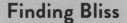

Your baby is *always* going to be on your mind, and knowing that can be a bit (okay, a lot!) overwhelming. Balancing your thoughts of your current baby bubble (feeding, napping, developmental milestones) with everything else in your life is also quite the challenge these first six months into your mommying journey. It can be a struggle to focus on other things or to just be in the moment while your baby is napping and your partner is talking to you. Trying to be present and have an intentional mindset is the best we can do, and there is no point in trying to label what is more important.

Once again, don't get a case of the "shoulds"—for example, "I really should be doing the dishes; I really should be engaging with my partner; I really should call back my friend . . ." All the "shoulds" will pull you out of the moment. On the other hand, you might find yourself feeling guilty if your baby-obsessed mind wanders away for a few moments. It's so hard to find a happy medium! Just remember, feeling distracted or entertained by something else is okay. You don't *have* to be consumed with your baby every moment of every day. This will also allow your baby to develop some independent coping and self-entertaining skills, which will be needed farther down the road. It's okay to know your boundaries when it comes to your balance and be firm with trying to maintain them . . . as well as your sanity. Be gentle with yourself, and give yourself grace. The balancing act is something all moms struggle with, so you are not alone.

DON'T GET A CASE OF THE "SHOULDS." . . . ALL THE "SHOULDS" WILL PULL YOU OUT OF THE MOMENT.

Knowing that I am a mom and CEO, people have often asked me, "How do you balance being a mom and working?" I think, *Hmm, I wonder if male CEOs/dads are asked the same question?* Nope. Never. After biting my tongue and running a few responses through my head, I respond simply, "F*ck balance. What does that even mean?" Balance seems to imply some equality between juggling multiple priorities. A better question would be "How do you stay present when juggling so much?" And the answer to that is, honestly . . . "It's really hard." I have to be intentional and mindful of what I am doing, whether it be playing with my kids or leading a meeting at work. But it certainly isn't easy, and I feel like it's a muscle I have to exercise all the time. I think it was my therapist who once said to me, "Yasmin, the amount of stress you take on to just schedule your exercise routine probably cancels out any benefit from the actual exercise." Suddenly, I realized I need to

THINKING ABOUT YOUR MINDSET, USE THESE PROMPTS TO REFLECT.

I feel frazzled or distracted when_____

_____

_____

_____

_____

_____

_____

_____

_____

_____.

I can remind myself to embrace the moment by _____

_____

_____

_____

_____

_____

_____

_____

_____

_____.

be realistic. I need a plan from the start of my day, and to not get frazzled if and when plans don't pan out. That old go-with-the-flow talk! Now when I look at my schedule for the day, I think realistically about how and when I can get things done and when I need flex time to roll with the unexpected. I've also noticed my energy and focus feel more limited in a way. So I've learned that it is best for me during the week to limit my schedule to work, kids, and maybe one night out with friends rather than having a jam-packed schedule each day. That's when I start to feel overwhelmed, spread too thin, and not really in tune with anything I'm doing. I've learned that trying to keep my mindset balanced works best not only for me, but also for those around me.

MAMA NEEDS SLEEP!

• • • •

Depending on how your feeding schedule is with your baby, you may actually be getting some sleep during this fifth trimester. Woohoo, go you! It's important to start healthy bedtime routines for you and your baby. Now is the time to go to bed early and not the time to binge-watch that Netflix show you've been eyeing until 2:00 a.m.! Sleep baby, whenever and, heck, *wherever* you can. Because soon enough, the little one will wake you up. You might have read that and thought, *Wait. I should be getting more sleep?* Just like a feeding schedule, sleep is different for everyone. Whether you are or aren't getting back to a regular sleep pattern, it's what you do prepping for sleep and waking that matters. Take the time before you go to bed to think about the things that went right that day. Remember something that made you smile. Put down the screens, take a few deep breaths, and let yourself fall asleep.

Easier said than done, right? Just like you will get your baby into a bedtime routine to encourage a healthy sleep pattern, establishing a routine works for us grown-ups too. Here are a few tips:

- Dim lighting an hour before bed.
- Take a warm bath or shower.
- Read or journal.
- Use blackout curtains.
- Find your coziness: use a weighted blanket, soft pajamas or blanket, or diffused essential calming oils.
- Be mindful about how you use your baby monitor, and limit other sounds or distractions.

In the morning, think about a few things you're looking forward to, things that are certain to bring you joy that day. Focus on the positive. If you're still struggling to sleep, continue catching a nap or two during the day when your little one is napping. You're not competing against anyone but yourself, so remember to be kind to yourself. Even if you just say to yourself each day, "I will survive," because you will!

I WANT TO
SLEEP LIKE A
~~BABY~~
TEENAGER
ON SUMMER
BREAK

YOUR MOODS

• • • •

Although you may have previously gone through times in your life when certain areas felt unpredictable, now you have multiple layers of unknowns. *How will my baby be today? What if they don't nap and I don't get to rest? How will my milk supply be?* Teething, sleeping, feeds, sicknesses . . . the list goes on and on. The hardest part during this stage is that you may feel like your mood and emotions are also completely unpredictable. There's no shame in feeling overwhelmed if that's the case or in wondering if you need help. The cliché phrase "one day at a time" suddenly feels like it resonates more than ever, because that is truly the only way to approach this stage of parenting. One moment at a time, one feeding at a time, one nap at a time may be just where you are at. Lean in to new healthy coping skills. When in doubt, take a breath and talk to a close friend or a doctor if you feel like things are just too overwhelming. Even online support can offer the help you need.

Think of three things you can control today. Everything else needs to take a back seat for now. Speak up and ask for help from your partner or village people to make sure those three things can become a reality.

Around the fifth month, we had to take Julian to the pediatrician for a checkup. Sometimes I still liked to sit in the back seat right next to Julian so I could be close to him. This time, as I was staring at my beautiful little dude, an old song I used to love, called "More Than Words," came on the radio, and I just started bawling. I couldn't believe there weren't words that could encompass how much love I had for my baby. I also felt a sense of shock that five months had passed—how did that happen so quickly? My husband asked me if I was okay, and I told him that if there was a word for being so happy and so scared at the same time, that was how I felt. A complete mix of every emotion. I told

THREE THINGS I CAN CONTROL TODAY:

1. _____
   _____
   _____

2. _____
   _____
   _____

3. _____
   _____
   _____

THREE THINGS I CAN'T CONTROL TODAY:

1. _____
   _____
   _____

2. _____
   _____
   _____

3. _____
   _____
   _____

him I didn't really need to talk about it; I just needed to release it, with tears and a ton of emotions. He looked at me, confused, and we went for our checkup. When we got inside, my pediatrician couldn't help but notice my just-cried eyes and asked if I needed any help. I told her I was totally okay, just feeling . . . a lot. So much! I was feeling overwhelmed with the lack of control over time and protecting my baby from everything negative in life, when he was just this little, innocent, perfect human. Thankfully, she validated my feelings and reminded me that in addition to this *giant* life change, my hormones were still adjusting, and if it continued, to reach out for help. Phew! I wasn't going crazy; I was just a new mom.

HELLO, ANXIETY

• • • •

Hopefully by this stage in your new-mommying game you're feeling more comfortable with this new phase of life and your little one is thriving. But can you actually relax? Can you stop your brain from swirling over all the to-dos to rest? Or does the weight of all the responsibilities you have now for your lil' one each day overwhelm you and keep you from ever feeling a sense of calm? It's hard to find time for yourself as a new mom, but it's *so* important for your overall health and sanity that you do. Whenever we feel spread too thin or like we haven't had a moment to ourselves, we naturally are filled with a bit of anxiety. Before you get to that place where your anxiety has you feeling like a volcano ready to explode, find a few things you can do to stop all that yuck. You may have to be intentional about finding a bit of zen in your chaotic, baby-filled days. However, you can do it, so whatever works for you, find that zen and avoid that anxiety volcano.

"Babe, what are you doing?" asked my husband as I lay there

staring at the baby monitor. It was 2:00 a.m., and I was addicted to monitor watching. "I can't not watch him," I said. It was true. I finally got my baby to bed, and I knew in my head that I *needed* to go to bed, too, but . . . I just couldn't. I couldn't turn my brain off or feel at ease enough to fall asleep, even though I knew my body was desperate for a few hours or even minutes of real sleep. Catnapping was my new way of life these first six months, and it really was catching up to me. But now my anxiety about all the things that could go wrong with my baby if I *did* go to sleep kept me even more awake. WTF!

Aside from the panic attack I had during childbirth, I had experienced anxiety only a few times in my life. But as the months went on, I found that at times a switch inside me went into alarm mode, and I would feel a strong sense of panic. It was typically soon after the sun went down and I knew a long night was ahead of me. Some nights, I just couldn't relax or sleep. I felt an extreme need to protect my baby at all times while also knowing that there was no way to actually do that.

Yep, time to press this one again.

Other nights, I could finally relax and surrender enough to allow my body to fall asleep and *rest*. I would describe myself as a super-prepared-for-anything kind of gal. But all this anxiety roller coaster riding? No. I began to realize these waves of anxiety were likely to be normal and I was going to have to find healthy ways of coping with them, and on some level, just accepting them. This inner battle, I learned, was unfortunately a part of being a new mom! It might dissipate some days, but it never truly goes away. It's that Mama Bear mindset that is just innately in us after we give birth, I guess.

Here are a few ways you can cope if anxiety starts to creep in. Keep in mind these are just a few things that work for me, and I'm not a medical doctor. If you need professional help with managing your anxiety, seek it out. Ain't no shame in that game!

- Let yourself feel the anxiety and find clarity in what exactly the root of it is. Is there anything you can do to reduce the worry?
- Allow yourself to go there. Yes. Think of the worst and remind yourself that you can get through anything; the chances of it happening are probably unlikely anyway. Catastrophic thinking isn't going to serve you positively in the long run. Squash that yucky thought up and throw it out!
- Talk candidly to a friend, family member, partner, or another mom friend. They might have some encouraging words that you need in order to put things into perspective and allow the anxiety monster to quiet down.

YOUR BODY

• • • •

Yay, the immediate post-birth yuckies are gone! At least I hope they are. I've always had body-image issues, and it was nice that during pregnancy and the first few months postpartum this wasn't an issue for me. Around this time, four to six months postpartum, I noticed two changes within myself.

#ThisChangedMyMomLife

Breathing

- Try to find five minutes to sit down and breathe in a room by yourself; use the nose to inhale for a count of four, hold for a count of seven, and breathe out for a count of eight through pursed lips.

- Try the Calm or Headspace apps (or any zen app you like) to have a guided breathing or meditation break.

Connection

- Find time with a friend or new mom.

- Talk to a therapist.

- Find a distraction.

- Pop into your fave home store and check out the goods.

- Binge-watch a light TV show.

- Listen to music.

Self-Care

- Take a bath; light candles.

- Journal.

- Make sure you are napping and getting enough rest.

First, I was still breastfeeding and had giant (for me) breasts, and it was new and felt awesome. I have to admit that having some cleavage was fun! It felt good to appreciate my body.

Second, I was so relieved that I had survived pregnancy and was no longer feeling like my body was aching, that I focused on ways to make my body feel loved by me. This came in two forms, with the first being getting massages every two to three weeks. I started with a massage therapist who was trained in prenatal and postnatal massage, but over time, I found a place close to me that did quick and cheap chair massage. OMG. Game changer. I could stop by there for a twenty-minute shoulder rub and feel like I had been cared for and could feel the impact of the massage. Were there times when I said grocery shopping was taking longer than expected so I could get a little rub? Well, yes.

The second way that I showed my body love was by building strength. This was partly because I could tell that holding my baby or toddler was putting such a strain on my back, and I had zero core muscles. So I hiked and did home Pilates; little by little, not only did I feel stronger, but the endorphins were oh-so-nice.

If you are like me, and so many who have body-image issues, use this time to reset your perspective. It will be worth it in the long run.

YOUR RELATIONSHIP

• • • •

Don't forget to make time for your significant other as well. Wait, who? Oh yeah . . . You've both been through quite a few ups and downs by now, and taking the time to reconnect is essential, even when you're still exhausted.

One thing my husband and I did during this phase, when we had a babysitter for a few hours, was leave the house and go for a drive. Sometimes we wanted to drive and listen to music or a podcast and have some quiet time while being together. Surprisingly, it was so enjoyable! It also allowed for novel and spontaneous stops, which is something I really missed from my pre-kid life. Other times date nights were great—it just depended on our moods. I guess the piece of it that I learned over time was to take the pressure off "we have to reconnect" because maybe we weren't so disconnected. Or maybe we just needed to hang as best friends. Or maybe we *did* need to have some deep talks about the ways in which we had changed in the last six months. Those first six months were very baby focused and, honestly, focused on me. There wasn't a lot of room to focus on my partner, who was also going through his own new-dad sh*t. For new dads, this time of change is also a reset. It takes courage to acknowledge and express how it feels being in these new roles. Communication is key!

YOU'VE BOTH BEEN THROUGH QUITE A FEW UPS AND DOWNS BY NOW, AND TAKING THE TIME TO RECONNECT IS ESSENTIAL, EVEN WHEN YOU'RE STILL EXHAUSTED.

So do it *your way* (meaning you and your partner's way) and adapt, listen, and recalibrate as needed. And remember: sometimes each of you may have different needs and expectations, so it's always good to talk about the plan when you get alone time, just you two.

YOUR VILLAGE

• • • •

Finally, after four or five months of being a mama, you may have more predictable times that you can hang out with friends or new-mom connections you've made. High five! For now, try planning walks or park dates, but always remember to be flexible and understanding with fellow mom friends. It's inevitable that one of you will be late, a kid will be sick or finally fall asleep in the car on the way to the playdate, and plans will be canceled last minute. All the unpredictable crap will come your way, and that is to be expected as new parents. Shit happens, so it's best to treat other parents with the grace you'd like to receive in the same scenario.

I remember trying to coordinate with other moms who had babies the same age, and it felt impossible, between nap schedules, feedings, the sniffles, or just being too damn tired! It was easier to begin to hang out with other friends who didn't have those constraints. I could bring my youngest, Kiyan, along to hang with my friends, and it actually felt more relaxing. I loved this time when it just felt easier and allowed me to get out of the house more.

MONEY STUFF

• • • •

Now that you are through the initial survival period, where comforts and convenience go a long way, it's a good time to check in on finances. Four of the key expenses to consider in the fifth trimester are:

1. **Childcare costs.** Whether it's a nanny, nanny share, or daycare, childcare is not cheap.
2. **Kid food.** They are eating! While it may still not be a lot right now, you will probably start buying foods specifically for your little one. You may opt to make your own baby food, or buy it ready-made at the grocery store. There are also some amazing baby-food home deliveries, like Little Spoon and Tiny Organics.
3. **Vacation/fun.** It's critical to keep up the fun and new experiences for you and your baby. It's also nice to have something on the books that you are looking forward to.
4. **Self-care.** Whether it's a Pilates class, massage, or time with a therapist, these are new or recurring expenses that can add up.

YOUR IDENTITY

• • • •

During the fifth trimester, I realized that I was learning more about myself than I ever thought possible. It was like all my values and beliefs were brought to the surface, and I had to face the fact that I had to be my best self in order to give the best me to my children. I wanted to give them that as their model, not some crappy version of myself.

Surprise!
The layers of who you are and why are going to rise to the surface.

It was a real "Oh f*ck" moment . . . knowing I had some work to do to get to be that amazing *me* I wanted and knew I could be. It's definitely a process and takes time, and hey, some therapy too.

In the meantime, my focus was on loving myself and my baby fully, as well as being mindful of attachment psychology: my own, my partner's, and how our style of parenting may affect them in the long run.*

Now, it isn't the time to get too stressed or overly analytical

---

*For more information on attachment psychology, see: https://www.verywellmind.com/what-is-attachment-theory-2795337#citation-8.

about all this, but it is good to know how behavior affects attachment. This is big-picture thinking, so don't lose your sh*t over a single day or moment when you just couldn't be your best self.

MOM GUILT

• • • •

One day during my first pregnancy, I was out to lunch with a good girlfriend who already had kids, and I mentioned how nervous I was about becoming a mom. I told her I was so worried I wouldn't be able to handle all the sleepless nights, the breastfeeding, the pumping, and just . . . all the mom stuff! And that it wasn't just the first few weeks; it was more than a few months. As an almost-forty-year-old, I had always had time to myself to recharge, and I was filled with terror. How would I be able to take care of myself and my baby? She looked me in the eye and said, "But you will." She said it so confidently, so simply. She said, "You will. You'll handle all of it, and you will be a great mom . . . You just don't know it yet. Something will kick in like a gear you didn't even know you had, and you'll mom like it's just second nature, because it is." She then proceeded to tell me to not start feeling any mom anxiety or guilt now. There would be plenty of time for mom guilt down the road! She sure was right.

And we *all* feel this. I don't know one mom who hasn't felt guilty for anything from self-care to working, both of which can be critical. During this fifth trimester is when I really started to feel those worries, the ones I initially had. This was now a time where feedings and naps were more predictable, so I could find little moments to myself or even ask for help so that I could go hang out with a friend, *but* then the guilt came on strong. And the voice in my head was saying, "I don't really need to," or "What if something happens and I'm not here?" But soon I realized I had to take those breaks and I had to find ways of not feeling bad about it. I noticed that even after thirty minutes or a few hours away, I felt refreshed and more excited to see my little cutie. And having that presence and energy helped to diminish some of that guilt.

#ThisChangedMyMomLife

I think the first alone time I had outside the house after having my baby was at Target. It was blissful. Seriously. I wandered the aisles for forty-five minutes alone, not thinking about anything and just enjoying the freedom (until my boobs hurt and I knew it was time to head back home). Needless to say, admit what you actually want for yourself. There is no one right way to do self-care.

WHERE IS THE BLISS?

• • • •

Let's face it—these first six months can be kind of a shit show, and it's hard sometimes to not focus on the struggles. Then someone tells you to be grateful, and you feel even worse. It's a good practice to not just think of a few things that fill your heart with joy but acknowledge them in the moment. Sometimes it's the tiniest moment, like your baby smiling or cooing back at you, that fills you up and reminds you that this is all worth it. Some days it may be your baby that brings the warm fuzzies,

MY MOMENT OF BLISS THIS WEEK WAS:

and other days it may be something *you* did that makes you feel amazing. Either way, cherish it and let it fill you up!

For me, it was Julian's tiny hand holding my pinky that made me melt. With Kiyan, my second born, it was him napping on my chest that was always a heart-warmer. As time went on, these blissful moments evolved, but they were always our little moments of affection. It brought a new warmth to me. These blissful moments reassured me we had a magical bond that was just ours and could never be duplicated. It was unique and fulfilling in ways I can't express. It was me and them, and the bond was unique to just us. I actually felt like a *mom*! Cherish these moments because before you know it, you'll turn around and this little baby will be getting their driver's license or heading off to college. These are fleeting, incredibly special moments, so savor them. (Oh, and it's okay to feel the bliss and feel pissed off two seconds later!)

CHECKING IN ON YOURSELF

• • • •

Just as you learned in the prior chapter, "The Fourth Trimester," it's important to keep up the self check-ins!

Hopefully now you are able to get out a little more and do some of the self-care that suits you best. And while it can be stressful to find the time or ask for the time, it's very much needed.

MY HEART AND MIND

THOUGHTS

O Am I feeling present and calm?
O Do I feel good about myself as a mom?
O How am I coping with the challenges?
O Do I feel supported?

ACTIONS

👍 Journal.
👍 Meditate or listen to a meditation.
👍 Find time alone to think and not think (always!).
👍 Spend time with family and friends.
👍 Talk to a friend, therapist, or partner.

MY BODY AND HEALTH

THOUGHTS

O Am I being patient and gentle with my body's healing process?
O Am I feeling stronger and motivated to move my body?
O How do I feel in my body?
O Do I feel healthy?

ACTIONS

👍 Cook or bake something delicious.
👍 Move my body, do yoga, or take walks.
👍 Get a shoulder massage (full-body may be a bit much for you at this time).
👍 Get sunshine; go outside (always).
👍 Have a bedroom dance party.

CHAPTER 3

THE SIXTH TRIMESTER

> **Baby:** From six to nine months
> **You:** Feeling like you own your body again, experiencing fewer unknowns and less stress, and being ready to be called "Mama" soon

Life with your baby is probably still feeling a bit surreal, and somehow six months have passed. You have been a mom now for six months—congrats! Hopefully the daily routine is feeling a little more predictable . . . which of course means that things are likely going to change. It was just as I was feeling settled that my brain began to think about what was next . . . Is it hard for you, too, to turn off your thinking about the future?

WTF IS GOING ON?

• • • •

While you may be feeling more settled in with some parts of this new life, you are still likely to be having at least five WTF moments every day. For me, I could feel a shift in my head where I suddenly had more space to think about my needs and wants and not just focus on the baby. Part of this was because I was getting more sleep and the days were less blurry.

However, this led to my needing more brainpower to make decisions and plans, despite many "WTF do I do" moments. My previous priorities began to swim back up to the top—my relationship, work, travel plans, etc. And how would the baby fit into all this?

To adjust to the overwhelm, I embraced the classic phrase "one day at a time," and it really worked.

MOM LABELS

• • • •

Just like the last few months, the pressure to have a mom identity is still looming. And if you are around other new moms, the topic of work and childcare is probably happening, which comes with its own mental load.

During the sixth trimester, I felt like I had to choose which label I was—either a working mom or a stay-at-home mom—and I hated that it felt like only two categories existed. You don't have to define yourself as a working mom or a stay-at-home mom—forget that. Just be you and own that right now. You are likely doing tons and still have a giant to-do list, regardless of whether an office or home is involved. The key is to not judge yourself (or any other mom) while you figure this out; it's okay to be unsure, have mixed emotions about it all, and be vulnerable with those around you. It will actually encourage other moms to do the same. And for many moms, there isn't a choice, and this can be a hard adjustment too. So let's drop the labels and judgments, because there is so much more behind decisions.

THE WORK DILEMMA

• • • •

You may be super ready to go back to work and excited. And nervous. And sad. Then you think, *Wait—maybe I don't want to work. Maybe I can negotiate for part-time. No, I can't handle the baby full-time. But maybe I can and will love it. I have to work—we need the money . . . but how much is childcare? Hmm.* This is your brain on "new baby," or at least how mine was!

All these emotions are typical. And yet we also have to recognize there are so many individual circumstances—single parents, divorce, children with special needs, new circumstances from COVID, etc.

You may not know how you want to spend your time just yet and whether your preference can be reality. Start the conversations now with your partner (or yourself) about finances, the cost of daycare, and what all the scenarios look like, and then go from there. Remember that nothing is permanent, so if you head in one direction but decide later you want to change course, you can. You just have to feel empowered to be the mom boss that you are.

The trickiest part of this time and the decisions you have to make is that things have changed drastically in your life. There are new things to weigh out and think about:

- If you are in a relationship: Are we both on the same page about income and whether we both do/don't need to work?
- What is the new monthly budget?
- Did I work before and love it?
- Do I feel obligated to return to a prior job, or do I want to?
- If I need to find a new job, how long will it take to find work?
- If I could work from home, would this change my desire and/or ability to work?
- What would childcare look like if I were to work? What is the cost for full-time or part-time?
- How can I think creatively about the next six months?

While my brain was spinning on what the return to work would look like, I knew I was returning to Mommy's Bliss because I loved it and, in all honesty, I needed it—the community, the mental stimulation, the financial security. I also had the privilege of flexibility and of having my husband bring the baby to the office for occasional feedings and kisses. As fortunate as this was, over time it got harder emotionally to see my baby in the

TO WORK OR NOT TO WORK, *IS* THAT THE QUESTION?

Do I want to or have to work? _____

My identity and feelings if I do work: _____
_____
_____

My identity and feelings if I don't work: _____
_____
_____

Our finances if I do work: _____
_____
_____

Our finances if I don't work: _____
_____
_____

Support system if I do work: _____
_____
_____

Support system if I don't work: _____
_____
_____

middle of the day and then get my brain back into work mode for three to four hours.

REMEMBER THAT NOTHING IS PERMANENT, SO IF YOU HEAD IN ONE DIRECTION BUT DECIDE LATER YOU WANT TO CHANGE COURSE, YOU CAN.

The bottom line is if you love working, own it! And if you love being home, own it! And if you like a little of both, own it! This is *your* journey. And while you may feel judged by others, it's your own judgment of yourself that you can change.

THE JUGGLE

• • • •

Transition time is here! Whether you are now adjusting to a work schedule or your baby's childcare schedule, some kind of schedule change is likely to be happening. Structure can feel good and predictable for some, while for others it can be stressful. It's possible that you are now spending more time away from your baby, so when you are with them, it may feel more natural to be present and aware of all that they are doing. At the same time, you may have other responsibilities pulling at you, so default back to lists and calendaring, and then block out the times when all you will do is be present with your babe and the times that you need to have self-care or alone time. (Side note: it's a good idea to do this with your partner too.) You just have to plan and make it happen. Sometimes your plans don't work out, and that's okay. The trick is to prioritize what you know you need and hold yourself (and those who can help you) accountable.

#ThisChangedMyMomLife

Prepare for the next day!

Mental prep: I usually look at my schedule in the evening for the following day so I know what to expect and get ready for. Instead of assuming I will squeeze in a walk or phone call, I look realistically at the day, and if something will be too stressful to fit it in, then I plan to skip it. Sometimes knowing the day may be chaotic actually helps it feel less stressful and makes me set some boundaries (even with myself!).

Physical prep: I look at what I can prep the night before if I have an early start. I choose clothing for myself, prep the extra clothes or supplies my baby may need, pack extra wipes and diapers, dry snacks for me and baby, extra Ziplock bags, etc. Of course, this prep depends on what is planned for the day.

YOUR BODY

• • • •

Your body has done amazing things in the last six to nine months, and you have survived. It's likely that the sore areas have healed and your organs are back in place. Yay!

Around this time was when my mindset slipped back to wanting to feel slim again, and that's when my mom reminded me, "It took nine months for your body to grow that tiny human; give it at least nine months to heal." She was right. I needed to be gentler with myself, and I began to focus on what felt good to me instead of thinking about my appearance or weight.

I've always loved being outside, but during this time, I truly embraced it with my baby strapped to me or on solo hikes. Just moving my body and feeling the sun felt so invigorating (thank you, endorphins!). Slowly building my strength back up felt like the right thing to do in this phase rather than working out in a gym. Plus, when I took my baby with me, it was such a special time and encouraged me to engage with him in different ways.

#ThisChangedMyMomLife

Embracing little joys. Did you know that you can buy a cute and comfy pair of adorable new undies at Target for the same cost as a latte? For some reason, buying new underwear, even one pair, was like gifting myself a new house. Clean, comfy, sexy, or cute, all of these factors made it worth it.

YOUR RELATIONSHIP

• • • •

Date night! What? Yep, you may actually leave the house and enjoy your partner's company, without your baby connected to you. The hard part is you (and your partner) may feel pressure for it to be super romantic and connecting. I think the first thing to do is let that go—having time together is just about that. Maybe sitting across from each other at a fancy dinner isn't what you are in the mood for. Try a long walk or watching the sunset somewhere with a bottle of wine.

And after you're done talking about how much you love your new baby, it may be a good time to connect on how different life is and whether you are on the same page about expectations. The fact is life has changed. You both have new responsibilities and a new level of exhaustion, both physical and emotional.

Take this time to listen to your partner and also reflect on yourself. Talking openly about all this can help you steer clear of resentments and make it easier to talk about all this again at another time.

- Are we spending enough time together as a family? As a couple?
- Are we each spending quality time with the baby?
- How is the flow of the day going? Do we start frazzled or organized?
- Are we sharing or agreeing on how/when the house is taken care of, and who does what?
- Is it clear who is taking care of meals, groceries, errands, etc.?
- How are we on managing the finances?
- Do we have the community and social fun we expected and want?
- What is something we both look forward to?

Since your brain may feel blurry when the time comes to plan a date, here are some suggestions.

CIRCLE YOUR FAVORITES!

Going on an
urban walk

Getting massages
together

Getting a drink at
a favorite bar

Going to a
comedy show

Eating out

Doing something
active outside

Picnicking

Having a long
snuggle and nap

Going to the movies

Chilling with a view

Taking a long drive

Playing a game

Going shopping

Checking out
a museum

Seeing live music

#ThisChangedMyMomLife

When I was at work one day, an Italian manufacturer was having some challenges, and it was clear we needed to visit the facility, which was in Italy. I immediately said that I couldn't go, because I had a nine-month-old baby. My Italian colleague laughed and said, "Bring the baby!" I laughed and then realized he was serious. And then it dawned on me—I could actually do real-life stuff with a baby! I had this mental block I had to push aside. And maybe it would be fun? After I thought more about it and talked to friends with kids, I booked tickets for me, my husband, and Julian. Everyone had agreed that actually this stage, when Julian wasn't walking and just being strollered around, was the perfect time to travel. And after twelve days in Italy, I could say that they were right. The eating and exploring were so fun and relaxed. Luckily, my meetings were minimal and only for a few days, so I could add some vacation days. It was a wonderful experience.

YOUR VILLAGE

• • • •

Once again, during the sixth trimester, your village is likely to be changing and, possibly, becoming bigger (which is a good thing!). This allows for more help, support, self-care, and fun! Does this mean life is busier? Yes. But it's going to be okay.

It's probably time to pull out the calendar and start mapping out the weeks. If you aren't a list maker, now is the time to become one! And if you have a partner, get them on board too. If you prefer to go with the flow and can do that, then do it!

I think the keys to this phase are:

- Figuring out what you need and how/when you need it
- Being honest with yourself: Who do you want to spend your time with?

Let's face it: some people in our lives can suck the energy right out of us. But we keep the relationship. Maybe it's not quite toxic, but you already have five excuses ready for bailing on them when the time comes. So this is a great time to honestly reflect on the core people who you want to be around and who enrich your life—with a few, and I mean only a few, obligatory hangouts mixed in.

Remember: you are the boss of your life! We have to keep setting boundaries and being flexible while pushing life forward.

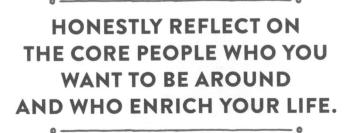

HONESTLY REFLECT ON THE CORE PEOPLE WHO YOU WANT TO BE AROUND AND WHO ENRICH YOUR LIFE.

#ThisChangedMyMomLife

Around months seven and eight, I realized that I was making too many plans, both fun ones and ones that felt kind of obligatory. And life with a baby was unpredictable. Of course, some of the other moms I was making plans with were in the same boat. Yet it felt like we didn't want to be honest when we just didn't feel up to hanging out.

That's when I started (gracefully) being honest with friends and family, rather than making excuses (where I usually blamed it on baby stuff). Now, I wish everyone felt they could give themselves and others permission to just say how they feel rather than bailing, making excuses, or showing up when you don't want to.

My go-to phrase for canceling plans was "I am so sorry to do this when we have plans, but I'm just not feeling up to it. Can we take a rain check?" Whereas setting a boundary sounded like, "I'd like to find time as well, but right now I am just enjoying being a homebody and spending time with only my family. I will reach out soon when we are up for more social time."

MOM GUILT

• • • •

Boom! It's back. That lovely feeling of guilt, for hiking alone, for going to work, for doing something that you have to or want to do. And it sucks. It's hard to remember that taking care of yourself is actually (1) making you a better mom and partner and (2) giving a gift to your child. You'll enable your child to learn to trust you, showing that you *do* come back after time spent away. Remember: modeling independence is valuable.

For many of my friends and me, the guilt was different in the sixth trimester because we could actually do more and be away for longer. Was it more guilt? Maybe it just felt different. At this phase, you and your baby know each other so well that the awareness of not being there is bigger for everyone.

But I knew I craved a break—time away to chill out, have fun, and sleep—and so I planned a night away. I had weaned Julian off breastfeeding around month six, and so now that he was around eight months, I felt I could do it more easily. The first few hours were so relaxing, and then after that, it was a weird combination of missing my little Julian like crazy and being so content not being needed all the time. And of course, I didn't friggin' sleep well at all. I had high expectations, not realizing my brain and body were not going to let that happen after months of interrupted sleep.

So, take the breaks. Know you will feel some guilt, but more importantly, you will be gifting yourself and your baby some independence.

REMEMBER: MODELING INDEPENDENCE IS VALUABLE.

WHERE IS THE BLISS?

• • • •

It's there! Now that you have seen your baby look into your eyes and smile, or found that everyday nap where you snuggle, the bliss is there. There is still a lot of adjusting to be done—not to mention the chaos and sleepless nights—but hopefully it is all feeling worth it.

I have to admit that the sixth trimester was my favorite time with Julian. With Kiyan, I loved the fifth trimester, since I snuggled with him so much. But with Julian, it was around months eight and nine that the giggles started and his little personality came out. Not to mention he was chubbier than ever.

The real bliss was that no matter where we were or what we were doing, I felt like his mommy, and he knew it. My baby brought a whole new purpose and meaning to my life. And I felt more like myself again, going to work and seeing friends, while also cherishing the mornings and evenings with my little dude. It wasn't easy, but it felt like it shouldn't be. I mean, I was raising a little person and discovering myself in this new role! But it felt right, and I felt grateful and fortunate for the life we were able to create.

CHECKING IN ON YOURSELF

• • • •

Since high school, I have often contemplated the psychology behind things, and when I became a leader at Mommy's Bliss, I saw how important this was to understanding team dynamics. Now, becoming a mom made this time of self-reflection even more critical to finding my way and my bliss. One practice that has helped me to self-reflect in a way that I can track is using an organized ranking of the key elements in my life.

If I were to think about the key areas of my life, how would I categorize them?

- Mind
- Heart
- Health
- Emotional health
- Spirit
- Relationships
- Body
- Finances
- Adventure/Experiences

If I were to rank how I feel about these areas of my life, what number from 0 to 10 would I give them (0 being low versus 10 being amazing/optimal)?

Now you give it a try.

TODAY'S DATE:

Mind 0 1 2 3 4 5 6 7 8 9 10

Do I feel calm and grounded? Am I feeling intellectually stimulated in the way I need? Where is my focus?

Heart 0 1 2 3 4 5 6 7 8 9 10

How would I describe my heart right now: full, happy, empty, divided? Am I feeling all the love in my life? How are things with my partner (if relevant)?

Health 0 1 2 3 4 5 6 7 8 9 10

How is my physical health? Do I have the amount of energy I want? Am I taking care of my health?

Emotional Health 0 1 2 3 4 5 6 7 8 9 10

How would I describe my mental health right now? Is this typical for me or different?

Spirit   0 1 2 3 4 5 6 7 8 9 10

Am I feeling connected to
my spirituality?

Relationships   0 1 2 3 4 5 6 7 8 9 10

Am I feeling close and
connected to people in
my life? Am I spending
time with the people who
nurture and support me?

Body   0 1 2 3 4 5 6 7 8 9 10

How do I feel in my body?
Where is my focus?

Finances   0 1 2 3 4 5 6 7 8 9 10

Is this causing me stress?

Adventure/Experiences   0 1 2 3 4 5 6 7 8 9 10

Am I living life? Do I need
to plan more adventure
or experiences, or am I
content?

CONTEMPLATING BABY #2

· · · ·

Well, this conversation can go a lot of different ways depending on your circumstances. Many of my mom friends have joked that they had selective memory of the newborn days because they couldn't believe they did it again. It's true—the way things went with the first tells you a lot about whether you are up for a second. Then age, finances, relationship status, community, and other factors come into play.

I knew I always wanted more than one kid, but when this deciding moment came, there were two factors for me that were top of mind. First, my age—I had just crossed forty, and this concerned me because of possible health risks for the baby and my energy to get through pregnancy and the first few years. Second, the thought of the torture of six weeks of daily injections due to my blood-clotting issue made me cry. But to think of not having a second baby also made me cry. So, with time ticking, I went for it, and I'm so proud of myself for getting through it. (Shout-out to all the moms who have had to self-inject for many reasons!)

So where does this leave you? It leaves you in a space where you need to quietly sit and reflect on what you desire and what's possible with your current body and life.

Consider these things:

- Your age
- Your partner's age (if a factor)
- Your child's age
- Your medical history
- Your level of support
- Your financial stability
- Your emotional stability
- The costs for infertility support or adoption (if needed)

HOW FAR APART SHOULD I SPACE MY KIDS?

OMG, this question comes up all the time. There are pros and cons to every age difference, and sometimes the spacing isn't a choice; it just happens. Don't ask anyone this question; you don't need anyone else's input. Just do what feels right for you.

CHAPTER 4

NOW YOU'RE A MOM . . . FOREVER!

Baby: Nine-plus months
You: Mama Goddess, you have arrived. In your groove. Moody, tired, but feeling like *you*.

Here we are—you have made it nine-plus months into your mommyhood journey, and now you are officially in the mom zone. No more trimesters. Labeling yourself as "postpartum" is totally up to you! Some moms feel they are in this category for an entire year, some a few years or just a few months, some forever. There is no actual time frame specified; it just means "the time after childbirth." Since our bodies are all impacted differently and we heal on our own time frame, it makes sense.

WTF IS GOING ON?

• • • •

Wait; my baby is already nine months! Time is moving very fast and very slow. How is that possible? While I am not one for clichés, I do like "The days are long and the years are short."

Even to this day, I look at my two boys, and while their toys and crap are everywhere, I think, *I'm a mom of two boys, really?* And even though I watched them come out of my body, it still feels surreal but also blissful—and still hard on most days. Raising a kid is no joke—it takes all of our emotional and physical energy. I am tired all the time. But just as our kids go through phases, so do we as moms. And at this phase, hopefully you are settling in even more to this new existence, and the unknowns are now slightly fewer. You are just *you* now; the pre-kid versus post-kid identity crisis is over.

THE JUGGLE

• • • •

Family, friends, work, playdates, birthday parties, dates, the house, the groceries . . . oh wow. It's a lot. Now is the time to really get into using tools to help keep your life organized *and* to schedule time for yourself (you will need it!). Is spending time by yourself new to you? I have always enjoyed time to myself—it helps me recharge and relax. In fact, I crave time alone; to me it means quiet, freedom, and space for me to be me. I think for a lot of parents this is something they have adapted to so that they can feel and think quietly. If having time alone makes you feel anxious or unsettled, now is a good time to dig into that and see what's beneath it (yes, reach out to a therapist).

I also really enjoy shopping and traveling alone now. It feels carefree, where the only schedule I am managing is my own and the only emotions I am handling are mine. I can truly look after just me.

Think about where you are spending your time and how stressful or enjoyable it is.

- When I look at the weekly calendar, am I excited or stressed?
- Am I making enough time for me?
- Does it feel like a give-it-50-percent kind of day, or am I jazzed to give all things 100 percent? If I'm half-assed with work or home tasks, can I be at peace with that and just be fully present with my kids?
- When I plan a day, am I thinking about drive times, longer naps, or other complications that may hinder a stacked day of activities and lead to frustration?

HOW DO YOU ORGANIZE AND PRIORITIZE YOUR TIME AND ENERGY?

WEEKDAYS Morning   Midday   Afternoon   Evening

#1 Focus is on:
(ex. baby, me,
partner, work,
daily prep,
feeding, etc.)

#2 Focus is on:

Me time:

What I need
help with:

WEEKENDS Morning   Midday   Afternoon   Evening

#1 Focus is on:

#2 Focus is on:

Me time:

What I need
help with:

#ThisChangedMyMomLife

Schedule time-outs! What? Gaps of time, like a time-out to breathe, give the kid and yourself a break, and reduce overstimulation. This was a practice I learned after a few weekends of stacking plans. It was *exhausting*. So instead, I learned to make sure I had gaps of time between things. I also tried to only have one activity per day on the weekend. Just say no to more than you want to actually do!

YOUR MOODS

· · · ·

While your hormones may have stabilized, this new life is stressful, and right now you are dealing with extra psychological strain, so stress, which can sometimes be something positive, feels negative for sure. Even if you are just hanging at home with your baby, there is still a ton going on—much of it stressful—and your mood may vary day to day.

Once again, it's important to find time to check in with yourself, and it takes effort to make that happen. But self-care is a must!

What does self-care mean? Time to take care of *you*, to let yourself know that you matter and have needs that have to be met for you to be the best version of yourself.

This can mean daily practices as well as other times where you plan something special. For me, my (almost) daily practice is to hike or walk alone for at least forty-five minutes. If I'm too tired to exercise, I like to treat myself to a massage or pedicure.

A biweekly practice is talking to my therapist. Other forms of self-care that aren't as self-focused can include spending time with friends, going to yoga, or doing something that feels like it's all mine and just for me. It could be as simple as enjoying a coffee and croissant with a good gossip magazine. It's also important to get away for a night or two once you have trust-worthy childcare and you feel comfortable leaving.

#ThisChangedMyMomLife

I remember how guilty I felt the first time I left my baby with my mom so that my husband and I could have a quiet night away. It felt so hard to relax, and I kept thinking about how Julian would feel with us being absent. I worried about *him* worrying! And he was only a year old. It wasn't until later that someone told me to remember that spending some time apart was a gift for my baby—it helps them find security with new people and reinforces for them that parents always come back.

HELLO, ~~ANXIETY~~ WORRY

• • • •

Well, the truth is you should befriend anxiety because it's going to stick around forever. In my view, the good news is that it somewhat changes from anxiety, felt in your whole body, to worry. I think of worry more as waves of mental preoccupation with something that could go wrong. Underlying all of our fear and worries is the general idea that something bad could happen to our children. And yes, this can be overwhelming. At some point, you accept the worries, because even if we do everything in our power to protect our little munchkins, bad shit happens. But for now, just focus on doing everything you can to be a responsible, protective, and mindful parent. And you are not alone in this—I think all parents live this; it's just part of parenthood.

#ThisChangedMyMomLife

I believe in mama intuition. I believe we are so connected to our children that we can sense when something feels "off" and makes us worry more or drives a decision that doesn't seem obvious to others. This is a superpower! Not that we are actually able to prove we are intuitive but rather that we have the power to decide based on whatever the f*ck we feel. I have owned this and decided I'd rather go with my gut feeling, even if that means changing course. And that's my prerogative as a mom. It's yours too.

When I was choosing a small daycare for my baby, we were touring one and were supposed to leave our baby there for a few hours as a test run. I suddenly felt "off." I couldn't pinpoint anything wrong with the place or the people, but I felt like something was telling me not to leave my baby there. While I have no idea what would have happened, if anything at all, I went with my gut feeling and told them, "No thanks," and we left.

WHY HELLO, WORRY MONSTER. YOU DON'T FRIGHTEN ME BECAUSE I'VE GOT THIS UNDER CONTROL! WELL, MOSTLY.

When it comes to ME, I commit to worrying less about
_____ by doing this: _____
_____.

When it comes to MY BABY, I commit to worrying less
about _____ by doing this: _____
_____.

I accept that I will probably keep worrying about _____
_____ but not let it consume me.

If I had a magic wand, I would reduce my anxiety about
these two things: (1) _____ and
(2) _____.

And if I don't have a magic wand, but I do have superpowers that I can enhance, they would be my ability to
(1) _____ and
(2) _____.

I need to set my WTF timer to _____ minutes when I am
dwelling on _____.

I believe _____% in my mama intuition. Regardless, I
plan to follow it by listening to my body and heart.

I only need a little more _____
to know that I can do this mom thing, my way.

YOUR RELATIONSHIP

• • • •

I have found that the greatest aphrodisiac (or gift a partner can give) is giving space and time! It's hard when you are sleep-deprived and have a baby koala stuck to you all the time to feel like you want to be affectionate or caring for another. But it's important to figure out how and when you want to have these reconnecting moments with your partner. It's time for both of you to accept that your relationship and priorities have changed, which means some recalibrating is needed.

REVISIT YOUR
LOVE LANGUAGES!

Say what? If you have read Dr. Gary Chapman's book *The Five Love Languages*, you are familiar with the idea that we like to receive and feel love in ways that are meaningful to us as individuals. We may also express our love in different ways, and it's important to know how your preferences can differ from your partner's so that each of you has your needs met.

The five love languages are:

1. Words of Affirmation
2. Acts of Service
3. Receiving Gifts
4. Quality Time
5. Physical Touch

I believe our love languages ebb and flow as relationships grow, but once you have a kid in the picture, it is a pivotal time when your needs from your partner change. I like that the five love languages provide an easy platform to start from and maintain communication around meeting each person's needs so that ultimately the love that exists there is felt.

This doesn't have to only apply to romantic relationships. It is also a great way to think about your relationship with your kiddo and to pay attention to what is meaningful to them as their personality develops. For now, as you probably guessed, your best way of expressing love to your nonverbal child is through Acts of Service, Quality Time, and Physical Touch.

WHERE IS THE BLISS?

• • • •

Ahh, there is just so much bliss! And toys. And strange wrappers and food and diapers. But really, you are doing this mom thing and doing it the best way that you can. It's hard, but you keep going. The bliss is that you have and will continue to see what unconditional love really means. The bliss is that you know how uniquely strong a woman you are.

Should you get a lot of "Thanks" and "You're amazing"? For sure. But do you? Not so much.

Should you get a party celebrating your milestones as a mom? Yes! But do you? Not really. Mother's Day is kind of a shit show. You just have to know how to celebrate yourself frequently and in meaningful ways. And ask for what you want!

I do get a little feisty sometimes when I think about how much we should be celebrated. And instead, how often we are shamed in many different situations (airplanes, restaurants, at work . . . The list goes on). About ten years ago, before I had kids, I was interviewing a candidate for a job at Mommy's Bliss. As I was going through her résumé with her, I noticed a gap between jobs of about five years, and I could tell there was something sensitive behind it. I asked her how she spent those five years, and she sheepishly said, "I was raising my kids." I looked her in the eye and said, "That's amazing. I hope it was a special time, and I imagine it wasn't easy either. You should add that to your résumé!" She smiled with relief.

I am proud to say that having moments like this led us to create a really supportive parent community at Mommy's Bliss where there is absolutely no shame when it comes to taking maternity leave or spending time with family. Instead, we celebrate it. We have employee baby showers, and we give paid time off to attend family/school events with your kids. We don't discount your pathway to a promotion because you went on maternity leave. And we give paid parental leave no matter the route to parenthood (biological birth, adoption, surrogacy). We

also give paid time off for pregnancy loss. I feel fortunate as a business owner that we can do this, and I wish more companies would as well.

Parents carry so much emotional weight and responsibility, and this should be celebrated and respected all the time. And even though this book is about moms, I certainly believe the dads should be celebrated in the same way.

So, keep celebrating yourself. You are forever a mommy—with evergreen worries, never-ending mom guilt, and tons of heart-melting bliss!

CHECKING IN ON YOURSELF

• • • •

Now that life is back in full force, it's really time to figure out how and when you can find time to yourself to check in. While I really like the chart in the prior chapter where you spend time ranking areas of your life, I know we don't really have time for that every day. And I strongly believe that every mama needs at least one hour to themselves every day, which doesn't include any chores or work. Just time that you choose what you want to do.

So how will you build this into the day and routine? And can you combine things? For example, I love to hike the hills around my house alone. Half the time, I just think and reflect, and the rest of the time I listen to funny or enlightening podcasts. After an hour, I feel super refreshed.

Here are some examples of things you can do daily or weekly. The key is to keep it up!

MY HEART AND MIND

THOUGHTS

○ Am I feeling present and calm?
○ Do I feel comfortable with my mom style and decisions?
○ Am I using tools to better cope with the challenges?
○ Do I feel supported?

ACTIONS

👍 Have quiet time.
👍 Read.
👍 Listen to music.
👍 Journal.
👍 Meditate.
👍 Call good friends or family.

MY BODY AND HEALTH

THOUGHTS

○ Am I feeling stronger?
○ Am I feeling connected to my body?
○ Is there consistency with taking care of my body and level of activity?
○ Do I feel healthy?

ACTIONS

👍 Move my body; join a regular class.
👍 Have a massage or get acupuncture.
👍 Meal plan with new goals.
👍 Make doctor or wellness appointments.

LEARNING AS YOU GO

· · · ·

I wish I had more wisdom to share as the years go on, but I'm just learning as I go. It seems a year or so goes by where you are labeled "postpartum," and then society sets you free to be a "mom" and make parenting decisions, manage all the stuff, and keep the little ones happy, healthy, and alive. You are still expected to know WTF you are doing, and the truth is you don't. None of us does. But what we do know now is that we have confidence in ourselves to do the best we can, use the tools that work for us, and surrender to the unknowns.

The one area that you can always own is your ability to love yourself and your kids, and while it sounds easy, we know it's not. But it is the one thing in our control and the most important thing to model for our kids. So be yourself and give yourself grace to just be *you*. **And do this mom thing *your* way because that's the only way.**

EXTRAS

· · · ·

YASMIN'S MUST-HAVES

Get ready! Prepare by stocking up with these must-haves for the first few months postpartum.

Mommy's Bliss Nipple Balm
I love that you don't have to choose between lanolin or a natural oil-based ointment because this has both! The lanolin is long trusted for protecting the nipples, while coconut oil and shea butter soothe and moisturize.

Medela or Lansinoh Nipple Shields
These may look and sound like a weird idea, but they can really help when you are in pain due to cracked and sore nipples.

Lansinoh Soothies Cooling Gel Pads
It's all about finding relief when your nipples hurt! These help soothe, heal, and create a barrier so you aren't cringing when you put your bra back on.

Lansinoh TheraPearl 3-in-1 Breast Therapy Pack
Sometimes you may get engorged or feel pain in your breasts, and while you communicate with your doctor about what's going on, this product is a great way to quickly help with pain in the meantime.

Mommy's Bliss Lactation Hydration Fizzy Tablets
OMG the *thirst*! I have never been so thirsty, all day every day, as while breastfeeding. Invest in a big water bottle and get these delicious tablets to boost your hydration while lactating. Mommy's Bliss is the first to make these tablets specifically crafted for lactating moms.

Mommy's Bliss Lactation Support + Probiotics
As we know, breastfeeding is a major project, and keeping up milk supply can be all consuming. Lessen the worry and have on hand natural support with probiotics and fenugreek.

Mommy's Bliss Lactation Support (Fenugreek-Free)
Since we know ingredients work differently for each of us, Mommy's Bliss now has a fenugreek-free option with mom-approved ingredients to also promote milk production.

Mommy's Bliss Postnatal Support Reset My Body
There's nothing like a little collagen and biotin in a yummy gummy to help with postpartum recovery. Your body has just been through a lot! And hair, skin, and nails need some loving, right?

Mommy's Bliss Postnatal Support Lift My Mood
I didn't know a lot about the plant ashwagandha until the past few years, and it's exciting to have a gummy that may help with mood. Of course, be sure to chat with your doctor if you think you need medical attention or medication.

Mamaway Bamboo Postpartum Belly Band
This band is a nice way to find that stable feeling when every-thing feels pretty jiggly. And while I didn't have a C-section, this is known to help while you heal.

Upspring C-Panty
This panty has a great silicone panel and is high-waisted, help-ing to support all the belly healing you may need.

PRO TIP

Although I am certainly biased, I am also a mom who used these two products and found them true lifesavers. I would have these already stocked in your cabinet for baby's arrival.

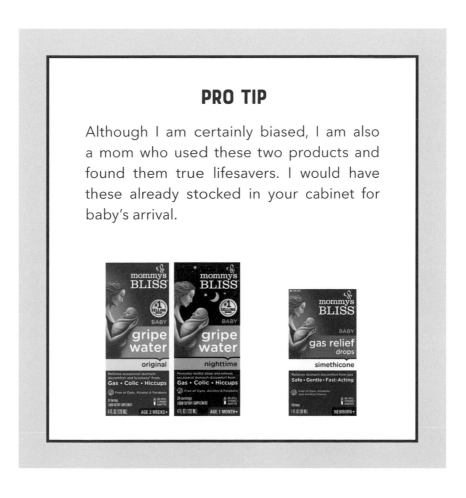

SELF-CARE, YOUR WAY

• • • •

I don't even think I had heard the word *self-care* when I was single or didn't have kids. And now here we are. People can't stop talking about it! It is so important to find these small moments where you can breathe and feel present. You are already taking care of so much, as well as a little human, that a little *you* time is worth it.

While it is difficult to find time to take care of yourself, let alone know what you need during the short breaks, here is an easy way to keep yourself accountable (with no pressure of course) to doing self-care *your way*.

My #1 way is _____.

My #2 way is _____.

My #3 way is _____.

USE THIS CHART TO TRACK HOW YOU ARE DOING WITH EACH SELF-CARE HABIT EVERY DAY FOR 30 DAYS.

Self-care habit #1:

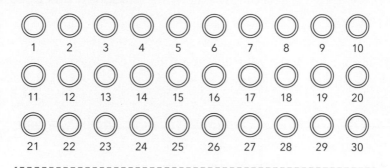

○ ○ ○ ○ ○ ○ ○ ○ ○ ○
1 2 3 4 5 6 7 8 9 10

○ ○ ○ ○ ○ ○ ○ ○ ○ ○
11 12 13 14 15 16 17 18 19 20

○ ○ ○ ○ ○ ○ ○ ○ ○ ○
21 22 23 24 25 26 27 28 29 30

Self-care habit #2:

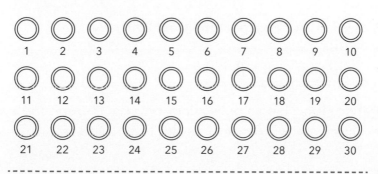

○ ○ ○ ○ ○ ○ ○ ○ ○ ○
1 2 3 4 5 6 7 8 9 10

○ ○ ○ ○ ○ ○ ○ ○ ○ ○
11 12 13 14 15 16 17 18 19 20

○ ○ ○ ○ ○ ○ ○ ○ ○ ○
21 22 23 24 25 26 27 28 29 30

Self-care habit #3:

○ ○ ○ ○ ○ ○ ○ ○ ○ ○
1 2 3 4 5 6 7 8 9 10

○ ○ ○ ○ ○ ○ ○ ○ ○ ○
11 12 13 14 15 16 17 18 19 20

○ ○ ○ ○ ○ ○ ○ ○ ○ ○
21 22 23 24 25 26 27 28 29 30

RESOURCES

• • • •

Now that your smartphone is part of your Postpartum and Mom Village, here are some useful resources. It's amazing how much has been created specifically for us during this postpartum phase.

Mommy's Bliss 360 is a great place to find resources, education, and community—all for new moms and created by moms. Find it at www.mommysbliss.com.

BREASTFEEDING: Find lactation support, anytime, anywhere
- https://nestcollaborative.com
- https://lactationnetwork.com

BODY

Nutrition and Postpartum Meal Delivery
- https://milkyoat.com
- https://nourishedfolks.com

Pelvic Floor: Find a pelvic floor physical therapist near you
- https://www.aptapelvichealth.org/ptlocator

Fitness
- https://mommastrong.com
- https://every-mother.com

EMOTIONAL AND MENTAL HEALTH
- https://prosperamhw.com
- https://postpartumhappiness.com
- Dr. Christine Noa Sterling, Board Certified OB/GYN, @drsterlingobgyn, https://sterlingparents.com
- Nicole Kumi, PhD, PMH-C, and CEO of The Whole Mom, @Nicole_Kumi, https://thewholemom.com

ABOUT THE AUTHOR

. . . .

Yasmin Kaderali is the CEO of Mommy's Bliss, a brand that offers over-the-counter health and wellness solutions for babies, kids, moms, and moms-to-be. Under her leadership, Mommy's Bliss has magnified its brand reach and has leveraged the experience of the parents on the team to drive product development and marketing. The company has successfully launched more than thirty new products in five years at national stores, including Target,

Walmart, CVS, and Walgreens. The company celebrates moms and has implemented progressive policies to support parents. Yasmin believes in moms' superpowers and that our culture should recognize that the major transition into new motherhood deserves more attention.

Yasmin holds an MBA from the Johns Hopkins Carey Business School, an MPH from the Johns Hopkins Bloomberg School of Public Health, and a BS in human development from UC Davis. When she is not busy innovating and bringing disruptive products to the market for mommies, you can find her playing with her two boys or hiking the hills in Marin County, California.